The Ways Children Learn Music

G-4355

The Ways Children Learn Music

An Introduction and Practical Guide To Music Learning Theory

Eric Bluestine

GIA Publications, Inc.
Chicago

Cover Design by The Kantor Group, Minneapolis, MN
Cover Illustrations by Brian Kantor, age 7
Book design by Robert M. Sacha

Bluestine, Eric, 1964-
      The ways children learn music: an introduction and practical guide to music theory /
      Eric Bluestine
            p.   cm.
      Includes bibliographical references (p. 166)
      ISBN: 0-941050-71-8
      1. Music—Instruction and study—Juvenile. 2. Learning.
      I. Title
      MT1.B665 1995
      780'.7—dc20   95-32684
                                                                  CIP
                                                                   MN

ISBN: 0-941050-71-8
Copyright © 1995 GIA Publications, Inc.
7404 S. Mason Ave.
Chicago, IL 60638

Table of Contents

A word about pronouns

I started out writing "he" and "him" every time I referred to my students, but I was bugged by the fact that half my students were being ignored. I then decided to switch back and forth with every new chapter from "he" and "him" to "she" and "her." A friend who proof-read this book in its early stages said that the constant switching of pronouns drove him crazy. I therefore decided to use only "she" and "her" throughout. If this strikes some readers as unfair, please be assured that I will use "he" and "him" exclusively in my next book.

E. B.

*H*ow many Americans are prepared for the musical experience? How many Americans can read music? How many Americans are even minimally capable of following the course of a Brahms symphony, to say nothing of a Mozart sonata, or even the finer points of a Gershwin tune? I would guess a fraction of one percent. Music desperately needs a prepared public, joyfully educated ears. Right now, music is an orphan; and it will always be that orphan until we get a grip on a methodology of music education for the young.

—Leonard Bernstein
From an essay entitled "On Education"
that appeared in Bernstein's book Findings.

*C*an I audiate most of the tonal complexities in music? No. I wasn't taught early enough in life to cope with them. So I do the best I can, and I keep plugging away at them each day. But I know my singing and my tonal audiation would be better today if I had received better instruction when I was younger. I doubt I would be as good as some other people; my tonal aptitude is not all that high. But if I had received proper informal guidance and formal instruction—who knows? I'm sure I would be a better musician today. Well, it's too late for me to do much about it for myself, but what can I do about it for my students? That's the nature of our profession—to make sure that our students surpass our level of accomplishment.

—Edwin Gordon
From a lecture on tonal syntax that
accompanied the 1989 edition of
Learning Sequences in Music.

*W*e all pride ourselves on having an open mind. But what do we mean by that? More often than not, an open mind means that we stick to our opinions and let other people have theirs. This fills us with a pleasant sense of tolerance and lack of bias—but it isn't good enough. What we need is not so much an open mind—readiness to accept new ideas—but an attitude of distrust toward our own ideas. This is the scientific habit of thought: as soon as you have an idea, try to disprove it.

—Rudolf Flesch
The Art of Clear Thinking

INTRODUCTION
Our Main Problem and a Possible Solution

The fault, dear Brutus, is not in our stars,
but in ourselves, that we are underlings.

—William Shakespeare,
Julius Caesar

I love children. I love hearing them laugh and watching them run and play. I love watching the looks on their faces when I sing a song to them in a tonality they've never heard before.

Also, I love teaching. I was born to teach. Some people don't know what they were born to do; I know. I feel very lucky that way. As it happens, I became a music teacher; but I think I'd be equally happy teaching something else.

Not long ago I delivered a sermon in a church. I spoke for only ten or twelve minutes, but I still managed to cover a lot of ground: I spoke about the Jewish people and their covenant with God, about the Jewish custom of celebrating Passover, about the various commandments we are called upon to obey. I spoke about the symbolism of the Jewish prayer shawl, about the various meanings of the Hebrew name for God. I used posters, visual aides. I had a blast.

But mainly, I was thrilled that I was speaking to *children*. It was a "children's sermon." Naturally, adults were present too. But my sermon was designed for kids. My impression was that they enjoyed

1

hearing it as much as I enjoyed giving it. (Who knows? Maybe I passed up a promising career as a rabbi!)

Also, I love music—more than I could ever describe. I listen to music every day the way other people eat food and breathe air. If music were to suddenly vanish from the earth, I would have no choice but to create it anew.

My career seemed to choose itself: *Teach music to children.*

Now for the bad news: Teaching general music in Philadelphia is not an easy job. Currently, I am teaching in two elementary schools, and I see roughly seven hundred children every week. I have just completed my sixth year as a public school music teacher. And I *still* love music, teaching, and children! My ongoing frustration is that *I cannot bring these three loves together.*

I suspect that my frustration is shared by most classroom music teachers. We desperately want to teach, but we are blocked by one obstacle after another. Here are just some of the many problems we face in Philadelphia:

- The dropout rate of music students in performance groups is alarmingly high.
- Music teachers are taken for granted and are thought of as second-class citizens in their schools by parents, students, administrators, and other teachers.
- There is no consistency or uniformity among music teachers from school to school; we teach whatever we please.
- Music teachers are woefully ignorant about existing research in the psychology of music, research that could help us to become better teachers.
- Music teachers do not even know who their colleagues *are*, much less what they do in their classrooms. (Music teachers in Philadelphia meet with their colleagues only once a year for one purpose: to discuss the up-coming District Spring Concert. What does this say about us? It says that we're more interested in

preparing for one concert, involving about 2% of our students, than we are in improving our teaching.)

All these problems are related; they stem from one basic problem:

We are not educating our students to become independent musicians and independent musical thinkers.

Here is a possible solution:

Let's design a music curriculum to help us teach better so that our students can grow musically and approach, maybe even surpass, our level of musical proficiency.

Certainly a new and improved music curriculum would not be a panacea; but imagine how far it would go in helping us solve our problems.

- Students who are developing a deep, meaningful, lasting understanding and appreciation of music will be less inclined to drop out of performance groups.
- If music teachers had a curriculum they could be proud of, they would never again accept second-class status.
- With a standardized curriculum, we could have both uniformity and accountability. Imagine what a thrill it would be to follow our students' progress from month to month, year to year.
- Music teachers would no longer be ignorant about existing research in music education. In fact, our curriculum would be *based on* existing research and would change and stay current in light of new research findings. (It's a curious fact that no one has changed or revised Philadelphia's "standardized curriculum" in at least six years. It contains the same typographical errors that were there six years ago. We're told, for example, to teach "simple sounds and canons.")
- Music teachers would have a *reason* to get together: Curriculum Development.

What's wrong with the standardized curriculum currently in use in Philadelphia? Simply stated, our "standardized curriculum" is neither standardized, nor is it a curriculum.

We are told, for example, to teach our second graders to "echo melodic patterns." Certainly this makes a great deal of sense. After all, tonal and rhythm patterns are the building blocks of music in the same way words are the building blocks of sentences. But which tonal and rhythm patterns should we teach? We're never told; and out of the hundreds of music teachers in Philadelphia, I doubt that even two ever choose to teach the same patterns. This is hardly what I would call "standardized."

We are told to teach musical skills (reading, creating, singing, chanting, etc.) and musical content (melodic contour, melodic rhythm, quartal harmony, etc.). The trouble is that these skills and content are strung together arbitrarily with no underlying logic to their sequence. First graders, for example, are taught to *read* music before they are taught to *understand it aurally*. This is hardly the basis for a workable curriculum.

Does all this sound familiar to you? I suspect that these problems are not unique to Philadelphia. Perhaps you'd like to revise the music curriculum in *your* school district. But where do you begin? What form should a new music curriculum take? In what ways should it resemble your old one? My belief is that before teachers and administrators can write a music curriculum—or revise an old one—they must first educate themselves about child development as it relates to music. In other words, they must understand Music Learning Theory[1] and the pioneering work of Edwin Gordon.

Unfortunately Music Learning Theory is a tough subject. Weeks, months of study are required to understand it well enough to use it; and even then, the music teacher's task is not completed since Music Learning Theory can never be understood fully. Why is this? Because Music Learning Theory is, as its name suggests, a theory of

---

1 I take my cue from Walters and Taggart (1989, p. v) who have chosen to capitalize the term "so that it can be identified easily as an entity rather than as a generic phrase."

how children learn music; and as a theory, it is subject to continual revision and expansion. Is it any wonder that many music teachers respond to the phrase "Gordon method" with a mixture of hostility and fear?[2]

I, too, have felt these emotions about Gordon's work. Understanding Music Learning Theory has been a slow process for me. When I started teaching music six years ago, I knew almost nothing about it. In fact, I'm embarrassed to recall that I thought of myself as a "specialist." In general, I confused three things: Music Learning Theory, methods *based* on Music Learning Theory, and teaching techniques. Let me briefly explain them.

Music Learning Theory is nothing more than a theory—or *collection* of theories—about how students learn musical skills and content most effectively. It's child-centered; that is, it's about how children learn and not about how teachers teach. Doesn't it make sense that teachers should understand how children learn *before* they decide how they're going to teach? But once music teachers understand how children learn, then they are ready to create a learning method—a series of sequential and comprehensive objectives. Look at it this way: Music Learning Theory is something you *think about*; a learning method is a step-by-step series of objectives that you actually *write down and plan to do*. And teaching techniques enable you to *carry out and achieve* your objectives.

Are you still with me? I've talked about three topics so far. Now imagine music education separated into *four* topics: 1) the musical and pedagogical principles that give rise to Music Learning

---

2 Edwin E. Gordon is a distinguished professor in residence at the University of South Carolina—Columbia.

As I will explain in chapter 7, there is no "Gordon Method." The term is improper and I, therefore, will not use it in this book. I will, however, occasionally use the term "Gordon Learning Theory" in place of Music Learning Theory. By so naming it, I do not mean to suggest that Gordon is the only researcher in the field of Music Learning Theory. It's a term of convenience, since he is the most widely known and most influential researcher in this field.

Theory; 2) Music Learning Theory itself; 3) learning methods; and 4) teaching techniques.

The relationships and differences between these four topics are mainly what this book is about. In Part One, I explain the philosophical underpinnings of Music Learning Theory, often in personal, somewhat idiosyncratic terms. In Part Two, I try to answer these questions: What are the differences between informal guidance and formal instruction in music? What actually is supposed to *happen* during each level of Gordon's skill learning sequence? How does one design a curriculum based on Music Learning Theory? Finally, I take you on a tour of my rhythm and tonal exercises, and I also offer suggestions for teaching tonal and rhythm patterns.

Let me conclude this introduction by admitting, quite frankly, that my rhythm and tonal exercises are far from perfect. In order for me to improve them, I need the advice and wisdom of my colleagues and supervisors. In turn, I hope the information I present here will give music teachers and music supervisors the foundation they need on which to build a new and workable music curriculum for their school system.

Eric Bluestine
Philadelphia, PA

Part One

Music Learning Theory

CHAPTER ONE
Audiation

Heard melodies are sweet, but those unheard
Are sweeter.

—John Keats
"Ode on a Grecian Urn"

In a delightful book about music notation called *Henscratches and Flyspecks* (1973), the folksinger Pete Seeger wrote:

> Music teachers sometimes *over*emphasize [Italics his] the importance of learning to read music early. Would you teach a baby to read before it could talk? Should a teen-ager study dance notation before learning to dance? Musicians need, in the beginning, to train their ears, their vocal cords, or their hands, and to develop *the sense of music that tells them when to sing what* [Italics mine] (p. 9).

In this paragraph, Seeger suggests two things to music teachers. First, children should learn musical skills in much the same order they learn language skills: they should hear and perform before they read and write. Second, children must develop two generic skills simultaneously: 1) performance ability and 2) "the sense of music that tells them when to sing what."

A convenient term that Edwin Gordon has coined to refer to this "sense of music" is *audiation*. Perhaps you've heard the word before. But what exactly is audiation, and how does it relate to performance technique? I could say that you audiate when you "inner hear" music with comprehension, but such an oversimplified definition probably wouldn't help you much. I could tell you that "audiation is to music what thought is to speech" (Gordon, 1993), but you'd probably tell me that Gordon's analogy is too vague.

Perhaps an analogy with another art form might help. I discovered this explanation of the relationship between visualization and performance technique in—of all places—a book called *I Am Not Spock*, by Leonard Nimoy (1975). He writes:

> I've played enough roles and have seen myself enough times that I can project my performance from the time I first read the script.
>
> I suspect that it's similar to what happens when a block of marble arrives at a sculptor's studio. When he first looks at it, sees the image inside the block and then starts to chip away to reveal it to the eyes of others, the ability to see it is his visionary talent. The ability to chip away the excess is his craft or technique (p. 33).
>
> I am constantly asked how I managed 'to keep a straight face' while playing the [Spock] character. In terms of actor's craft it was easy. I'm always amazed at the speed and deftness with which a plumber fixes a leaky faucet. That's his craft. Mine included emotional control and manipulation.
>
> I was so thoroughly immersed in the character that my weekends were a gradual trip back to emotional normalcy. Or as close as I could get to it. By Sunday afternoon I would become aware of a lessening of the Spock presence. I would begin to relax into a somewhat more responsive state (p. 37).
>
> I am still affected by the character of Spock. Of course, the role changed my career. Or rather gave me one. It also affected me very deeply and personally, socially, psychologically, emotionally. To this day I sense Vulcan speech patterns, Vulcan social attitudes, and even Vulcan patterns of logic and

emotional suppression in my behavior.

What started out as a welcome job to a hungry actor, has become a constant and ongoing influence in my thinking and lifestyle (pp. 22-23).

Practically all you need to know about audiation is packed into this incredible excerpt. Let me go over some of the highlights.

First, we read about the phenomenon of Leonard Nimoy "projecting" a performance, that is, performing the play in his head. Pure audiation! Haven't you ever done that with music? Haven't you ever "performed" a piece of music in your mind? Of course you have, many times. What have you noticed at those moments? You may have noticed that the music in your mind was not proceeding at the same speed that it normally takes to perform it. You may have audiated a three-minute song in thirty seconds. You could do this because, when you audiate a piece of music, you don't audiate every single note the composer wrote.

This may seem strange to you. After all, when you perform a piece of music, you perform every note, and you do so in actual time. You may even *memorize* every note. But you don't *process* every note. Your brain chooses the important stuff, the highlights, the essential pitches and durations that make the piece what it is—in your opinion. Of course, the tonal and rhythm patterns in a piece of music that *you* think are essential may not be the same patterns that *I* think are essential. Getting tricky? Let's move on.

What about the block of marble in the sculptor's studio that Nimoy writes about? Several things are happening with that block of marble. The artist is seeing, visualizing, predicting the final product even before the actual work is begun. The same thing happens in music. If you're actively listening to a piece of music, then you're predicting what will happen next, even if you've never heard the music before!

And what is the basis for your predictions? Your past experience. Notice that Nimoy can project his own performance from the first time he reads a script only because he has seen himself so many times on the screen. Think about this in connection with music. The more music you've heard and the larger your vocabulary of patterns in various tonalities and meters, the better you can audiate. (How wonderful it would be if our students reached the point where they began asking these questions: How is the piece of music I'm hearing now similar to the piece I heard last week? Last month? Last year? How is it different?)

Something else might also be happening with that block of marble that Nimoy doesn't talk about. Imagine that the sculptor is half-finished with his work. Does he still visualize the same finished product that he did when he started? Probably not. In his mind, he has probably made subtle adjustments so that his visualization is slightly different than it was at first. As he looks at the block of marble in its constantly changing forms, he gains insight into what the work of art might eventually look like.

So it is with music. The more we listen, the more we try to discern the overall structure of the piece we're hearing. Our reaction as we're listening might be something like, "Aha! The lydian mode. Where did *that* come from?" or "Wow! I never expected that modulation to the submediant. Beethoven really *was* a genius."

Back to Leonard Nimoy. Notice that he didn't merely *play* the Spock character; he internalized it. In the same way, a musician who audiates must internalize music and not merely imitate it or memorize it. Imitation—even *perfect* imitation—is shallow and fleeting. By contrast, Nimoy felt the presence of the Spock character years after he finished his work on the *Star Trek* television series.

Finally, is audiation the same as "inner hearing?" Not exactly. Even though audiation *involves* "inner hearing," it doesn't end there. After all, Nimoy didn't merely "inner hear" his lines and then recite them; he became a character and then spoke as that character. To audiate music, our students must do more than "inner hear" sounds: they must process musical information. And to do that, they must learn to understand music. A lifetime job.

CHAPTER TWO
Whole-Part-Whole

*The true search for knowledge is not like the voyage
of Columbus, but like that of Ulysses.*
—Ludwig Börne

P *"The Art of Becoming an Original Writer"*

atterns, patterns, and more patterns.
Tonal patterns. Rhythm patterns.

These are what most music teachers think of when they hear the phrase Music Learning Theory.

And certainly, if we in Philadelphia were to write a new curriculum based on the principles of learning theory, a major part of it would involve tonal and rhythm pattern instruction. But you may be wondering: Why this emphasis on patterns? There's no simple answer to this question; and, in fact, I do my best to answer it in detail in chapters five and six. For now, let me just say that we do not audiate individual pitches or durations. Rather, we audiate music by organizing pitches and durations into *aggregations* of pitches and durations that become tonal and rhythm patterns. As we learn to understand how these patterns interrelate, we gradually learn to understand music.

But this answer only leads to more questions such as: Which tonal and rhythm patterns should we teach? How should we teach them? How does pattern instruction fit into our overall educational agenda? What are the advantages for students who receive pattern instruction?

Critics of Music Learning Theory often pose this last question, but do so with negative implications.

Atterbury (1992, p. 599) has written: "Considering the brief amount of instructional time for music in our schools, the efficacy of drilling on repeated tonal and rhythm patterns should be carefully considered."

Colwell and Abrahams (1991, p. 32) state the matter even more sharply. They suggest that "Gordon's teaching ideas are among the more elemental, focusing on the mastery of rather small patterns."

Edwin Gordon's response (1991, p. 72): "Students do not 'master' patterns. . . .They *audiate* them." Unfortunately, this terse rebuttal only muddies the waters for serious students of Music Learning Theory; it serves to inflame rather than to illuminate.

Advocates of Music Learning Theory understand that pattern instruction activities and traditional classroom activities (rote songs, circle games, etc.) are separate, but still complementary. Ideally, they should reinforce each other. How? Ah, how indeed! To answer that question, I must reveal one of the great secrets in music education, the awesome phenomenon known as

THE WHOLE-PART-WHOLE LEARNING PROCESS

There's no doubt in my mind: If you want to understand how to coordinate pattern instruction with traditional classroom activities, you must first understand the whole-part-whole learning process. Perhaps the most eloquent writer on this subject is Walters (1987, 1989, 1992), who summarizes the three stages as follows:

1. Introduction—Overview of the whole;
2. Application—Specific study of the parts (patterns);
3. Reinforcement—Greater understanding of the whole.

The natural, common-sense sequence is: Students learn a rote song; students hear and then sing or chant patterns (though not necessarily the same patterns found in the rote song); students return to the rote song with a greater understanding of its structure. This is how I work. It may strike you as odd that I dig into the parts of a

14

rote song by teaching patterns that are different from those found in the rote song. Let me say two things about that.

First, the patterns I teach are not altogether different from those found in the rote song. Virtually every rote song I teach is made up of tonal patterns with tonic, dominant, and subdominant functions—the same harmonic functions of the patterns I teach.

Second, it's important to remember that music teachers don't teach patterns so that children can "get the song right." That's merely a short-term goal. Children are taught to understand the musical elements in a rote song so that, eventually, they might understand those same musical elements in great music. The rote songs and the patterns we teach are means to that end.

Is there one "right way" to design a lesson that incorporates pattern instruction? For that matter, is there only one correct way to teach music? Certainly not. Teachers should devise their own techniques for teaching patterns. Also they should select classroom activities that, together with pattern instruction, form the content of each lesson. Finally, they should coordinate traditional classroom activities with pattern instruction so that the two reinforce each other.

How much class time should a music teacher devote to pattern instruction? Gordon recommends that teachers should teach patterns for only the first ten minutes of a class period; the rest of the period should be spent on rote songs and traditional activities. (I prefer to teach patterns sporadically throughout a period—two minutes here, two minutes there—instead of in one ten-minute chunk.) Clearly, there's a delicate balance at work here: teachers should *never apologize* for teaching patterns. After all, pattern instruction is central to the whole-part-whole process. And yet, how much of it is too much? At what point does pattern instruction interfere with the most important aspect of a music lesson—namely, music? Again, there's no simple answer to this question. As a music teacher, you must rely on your own instincts and coordinate pattern instruction with traditional activites in a way that feels right for you. As you do so, you might want to keep this in mind: pattern instruction (specific study of the "parts") is clearly not an end in itself; but without it, the chances are slim that your students would ever experience the payoff that comes at the reinforcement stage.

Pattern instruction actually serves three purposes: 1) It's a central element in the whole-part-whole learning process; 2) it gives music teachers a chance to hear children sing and chant *individually*; and 3) it gives music teachers accountability. Let me explain these last two points.

Imagine that you're teaching a math lesson. Imagine further, that you ask your *entire class* to solve the same math problem collectively. What do you suppose would happen? Naturally the brighter math students would carry the weaker ones. The same thing happens in music when we ask our whole class to sing and we never ask individual students to sing. The best singers do all the work; the others feel frustrated and they usually lip-synch.

But—and I can't say this forcefully enough—our job as music teachers is to teach *all* our students, not merely the brightest or the most talented. And pattern instruction helps us do that. Here's an example of what I mean. The procedure for teaching tonal patterns is: you establish tonality; you sing a two-note or three-note pattern; you call on one student to sing it back in echo; the student does her best; you make a note of whether or not she got it (Aha! Accountability!); and you quickly move on to another student. That's it.

Are most children embarrassed by having to sing or chant even a short pattern by themselves? Sure, at first. But once *you* get good at it, once *you* learn to move quickly from student to student, *they* will get over their fear and embarrassment, especially when they realize that everyone else in the class must sing and chant alone as well. The wonderful thing about these call-and-response activities is that they give every student a chance to grow musically in a non-threatening way.

My music lessons generally have a whole-part-whole structure to them in several respects. Not only do I proceed from rote songs to patterns, and back to rote songs again; I also have children sing as a group, then as individuals, then as a group again. This does wonders for their performance ability. It also confirms an idea that I have always suspected was true: children learn far more about how to sing from listening to *other children* sing in solo than they learn from listening to an adult—male or female—sing in solo.

Think about the whole-part-whole learning process in connection with our main problem—that we are failing to educate our students to become independent musicians and musical thinkers. Why is this so? Because we don't follow through with the whole-part-whole learning process. We finish the first "whole" by teaching a rote song, and then we get stuck; we don't know how to dig into the "parts." Pattern instruction, a cornerstone of Music Learning Theory, can help us correct this problem. It can help us create order out of chaos.

At this point, you may be eager to plunge into pattern instruction with your students. Certainly I would never discourage you from doing that, but let me give you one piece of advice: **Don't begin pattern instruction until your students are ready for it**. In other words, don't gloss over the first "whole." Expose your students to lots of songs in different meters and tonalities before you begin to teach patterns. Spend several months, maybe a year or two, on the first "whole." And while you're at it, test the waters: Call on individuals to sing fragments of songs. Listen carefully to their responses. Your hardest job will be to quiet down the rest of the class during these moments. But if you can manage that, you're on your way.

One last thing: Perhaps you're saying to yourself, "There must be more to Music Learning Theory than just rote learning and pattern instruction. If so, what is it?" Patience. You'll find out soon enough. For now, instead of telling you what Music Learning Theory *is*, I will tell you what it is *not*. It is not some magical force that will somehow solve all our problems. In fact, it's not something that "will work" or "will fail." One of the recurring themes of this book is that Music Learning Theory is nothing more than a collection of ideas—damn good ideas, but ideas nonetheless. It's up to us to make those ideas work.

CHAPTER THREE
Music Aptitude and Individual Differences

What a humiliation for me when someone standing next to me heard a flute in the distance and I heard nothing, or someone heard a shepherd singing and again I heard nothing. Such incidents drove me almost to despair; a little more of that and I would have ended my life—it was only my art that held me back. Ah, it seemed to me impossible to leave the world until I had brought forth all that I felt was within me.

—Ludwig van Beethoven
"Heiligenstadt Testament"

So far, I've discussed three basic issues that we should keep in mind as we design our new curriculum. 1) Our ultimate goal is to teach children to become independent musicians and independent musical thinkers. 2) Children must develop two basic skills simultaneously that will serve as readinesses for all future music learning: the ability to audiate and the ability to perform. 3) It's morally reprehensible for us to teach only the "most talented" students. All children have a right to learn music; and we must become aware of their individual musical strengths and weaknesses in order to meet their individual musical needs.

All this sounds simple, doesn't it? But how do we meet the needs of all our students? How do we teach them to audiate and to perform? Where do we begin?

We begin by acknowledging that all music students do not have equal musical ability. Some students learn quickly, while others need more time; some learn tonal content quickly and have trouble learning rhythm content, or vice versa; a few students have trouble learning both tonal *and* rhythm content; and a few students sail through pattern instruction with little or no trouble.

How do we assess each student's musical strengths and weaknesses? Certainly we should listen to our students sing and chant individually to learn about their tonal and rhythm *achievement*; but it's also important that we learn about each child's *potential to achieve* in music. That way, we can plan ahead as we organize our lessons. Not only can we react, on the spot, to the way our students perform; we can anticipate future difficulties they might have.

The trouble is that a child's potential to achieve is not something teachers can see or hear. A teacher can say, after hearing a child chant rhythm patterns correctly, "Wonderful! She's achieving." But a child's *potential* to achieve is, by its very nature, invisible and inaudible. What we need, therefore, is an objective measuring tool that can "hear what a teacher cannot see" (Gordon, 1993). Fortunately, there *is* such a measuring tool. It's called the *Intermediate Measures of Music Audiation* (Gordon, 1982), or IMMA for short, and it's an objective music aptitude test.[3]

I've administered the tonal portion of IMMA to over one thousand children at this point, and I have some interesting data that I'd like to share with you. But before I do that, let me give you some details about the nature of music aptitude that Edwin Gordon (1987) has discovered through his research.

1. Music aptitude is a product of both innate gifts and environmental factors, nature and nurture. Children are born with a certain degree of music aptitude. If they grow up in a poor musical environ-

---

3 Gordon has written five music aptitude tests that are designed to be administered to students of various ages, from pre-school age to college age. Since the students I test are between six and eleven years old, the most appropriate aptitude test for me to use is the Intermediate Measures of Music Audiation (IMMA).

ment, their level of aptitude—their potential to achieve in music later in life—will decrease. It's highly probable that a child's level of music aptitude is at its highest when she's born, and it decreases shortly after birth due to a lack of a nurturing musical environment. (Imagine how much a child's language aptitude would decrease if, after birth, she were not exposed to an environment rich in spoken language.) Perhaps, if the child is exposed to a rich musical environment, her aptitude level may increase to the point that it was when she was born. But it will never increase beyond that level. It will, however, fluctuate with the quality of her musical environment. Walters (1991, p. 68) sums up this phenomenon very neatly when he writes, "Young children are constantly changing their relative positions in terms of musical aptitude, depending upon the kind of 'nurture' that is interacting with their 'nature.'"

2. As children grow older, their level of aptitude fluctuates less and less until it eventually stops fluctuating. It stabilizes. That is, environment no longer affects a child's potential to achieve in music. This occurs when children are roughly age nine. Let me emphasize that students can still achieve in music beyond age nine regardless of whether they have high, average, or low aptitude. Nevertheless, this phenomenon highlights rather dramatically the importance of giving young children the best music instruction we can give them before they are nine years old.

3. There is virtually no relationship between music aptitude and intellectual ability, or between music aptitude and academic achievement. This doesn't mean that those with high music aptitude, by nature, have low intelligence. It means that one cannot be predicted from the other. Let me give you a striking example of this. I mentioned earlier that I have administered the tonal portion of IMMA to over one thousand students. The test is made up of forty questions. So far, only seven students have answered every question correctly. Of those seven students, two are mentally gifted, four appear to have average intelligence, and one is in a special class for learning disabled students.

4. Music aptitude is multi-dimensional. Gordon discovered that there are at least twenty different music aptitudes, and his *Musical Aptitude Profile* (MAP), a test for stabilized music aptitude, measures seven of them: melody, harmony, tempo, meter, phrasing, balance, and style. IMMA measures only two different aptitudes: tonal and rhythm. Why the discrepancy? Gordon (1991, pp. 68-69) states, "I do not accept simply at face value that the tonal and rhythm dimensions are the two major components of developmental music aptitude. It was found in research in the development of the test that the measures associated with timbre, loudness, and preference were too unreliable to be of use. As a result, only the two most reliable measures, tonal and rhythm, were used."

One fascinating aspect of music aptitude is that a child may have high tonal aptitude but low rhythm aptitude, or vice versa. Rarely do children have high tonal and high rhythm aptitude, or low tonal and low rhythm aptitude. If one aptitude level is high, the other is likely to be average or low; if one aptitude level is low, the other is likely to be average or high.

5. Music aptitude is normally distributed among the population. As Rudolf Flesch puts it, "People are, on the average, average." But we shouldn't overlook those students who have extremely high or extremely low music aptitude.

Possibly the thought that some students have low music aptitude bothers you. I feel the same way. How wonderful it would be if all our students had at least average aptitude. But this cannot be. Some students that you test *will* have low music aptitude; and, all other things being equal, a child with high music aptitude will achieve more in music than a child with low music aptitude. And that's that.

But you may say, "Wait a minute! You're discussing *quantitative* music achievement. What about individual creativity? What about artistic expression? What about motivation?" Yes, regardless of aptitude, everyone has something unique to express artistically. Yes, a child with low aptitude and high motivation may reach a higher level of musical achievement than a child with high aptitude and low motivation. Yes, an aptitude score is only part of the story. And yes, the *second* worst thing we can do is to take those damn scores too seriously. But the *very* worst thing we can do is not to take the scores seriously at all.

Now that I've given you some background about music aptitude in general, let me share with you my experiences with the IMMA test.

Due to budget cuts in the Philadelphia School System, I've taught in six different schools in the last six years. The one advantage to being bounced around is that I've been able to test children from all over the city. The total number of children tested, the age groups, the mean scores, and the standard deviations are shown in Table 4 at the end of this chapter.

For those of you interested in converting raw scores to specific percentile ranks, I've calculated percentile rank norms that you can find in Table 1 at the end of this chapter. Personally, I find the information in Table 1 rather gratuitous. Does it really help me to know that one child scored at the 51st percentile while another child scored at the 56th percentile? After all, both children have average aptitude.

What I do, instead of finding their specific percentile rank, is make a note of their *general* aptitude level: high, high average, average, low average, or low. I've made arbitrary cut-off points that can be found in Table 2. Students who scored between two arbitrary percentile points were classified as having a particular level of aptitude. This simplifies things considerably. I can go directly from raw scores to general aptitude levels. All the information I need is in Table 3.

Many music teachers I've talked to are highly suspicious of aptitude testing. The biggest fear seems to be this: If we label children as having high, average, or low aptitude, then that label will influence our teaching to the point where we will begin to stigmatize children. An aptitude score might turn into a self-fulfilling prophesy. We might even stop thinking of our students as children, and start thinking of them instead as numbers in a table.

I have some rather strong opinions on this subject. I believe, quite frankly, that our fear is justified. There *is* a danger that we may misuse the aptitude test and label children, and even deny them music instruction because of their low scores. How do we avoid this danger? By keeping three key points in mind.

First, we should remember that an aptitude test does not *cause* a child's level of aptitude; it *reveals* it.

Second, we should remember that it is our responsibility to choose *not* to stigmatize children. The test will reveal what it reveals. How we react to that information is entirely up to us.

Third, we should remember that irresponsible teachers, those who are inclined to label children and deny them instruction, do not need a test to justify their actions. Even the best music teachers fall into this trap. How many times have we lavished attention on some students and virtually ignored others?

I often think of this in connection with our District Spring Concerts. Please don't misunderstand me. I'm certainly not saying that we who invest so much time and effort into putting on these wonderful concerts are behaving irresponsibly or unethically. But consider this: Twelve children from every school participate in these concerts. If there are approximately six hundred children in every school, then approximately 2% of our students participate.

Now then. Two percent of our students get several days off to come to special rehearsals; two percent of our students receive special instruction and attention from at least *five or six* music teachers during these rehearsals; two percent of our students dress up and appear on stage in front of several hundred parents; two percent of our students receive thunderous applause after they're finished singing; two percent of our students receive certificates of congratulations. And two percent of our students feel great about themselves. Wonderful! BUT WHAT ARE WE DOING FOR THE OTHER 98 PERCENT?

A colleague once said to me, "I make sure that every student goes up on stage to perform at least once during the school year, whether they can sing in tune or not." Certainly that's admirable, but it isn't enough. Our job as music teachers is not to put kids up on stage and make them *stars*. Our job is to teach music by involving our students—*all* our students—in *many* different activities such as composing music, improvising music, and without doubt, performing music on stage.

An aptitude test can help us do this. According to Gordon (1993), music teachers should use aptitude tests for three purposes:

1. Aptitude tests should be used to monitor the developmental aptitude of children younger than ten years old. If a child scores, say, at the 70th percentile one year and at the 50th percentile the next, that means that her musical needs are not being met. Clearly it would be impossible for a teacher to know this without an objective measure. This may be one reason that so many music teachers resist aptitude testing. An aptitude test score can wake us up, but, as Maurice Samuel put it, "Nobody loves his alarm clock."

2. Aptitude tests can help us to meet the individual needs of our students. I'll explain some ways of doing this in the third part of this book.

3. With an aptitude test, we can discover those children who have high aptitude; and we can then encourage them to join our performance groups. **Again, we should never exclude students because of their low scores; but it would be equally wrong not to encourage students with high aptitude to participate in our choir, band, or orchestra.**

Let me conclude this chapter by saying that an aptitude test can help us in one other way that Gordon only touches on. Take a look, once again, at the bottom of table 2. You'll see that I arbitrarily defined a score of low aptitude as being between the 1st and the 20th percentile. There is no zero. Think about that: THERE IS NO ZERO! No child is without musical ability; every child has some music aptitude; every child can benefit from music instruction; and therefore, every child *deserves* music instruction. You may say, "Well sure. I've always believed that all students were educable. I've always believed in the democratic ideal of 'education for all.'"

But notice that your beliefs are just that: they're merely beliefs, ideals, abstract values. An aptitude test can change that. Somehow the test itself—the worksheets, the scoring masks, the instruction manual, the percentile rank that you write at the top of every test—transforms your abstract, democratic values into *physical, tangible reality*. Perhaps this is the most important thing that an aptitude test can do for us. Ultimately, it can do more than help us meet the individual needs of our students: it can meet *our* needs by redeeming our democratic identity.

Table 1
Tonal IMMA Percentile Rank Norms for Age Groups

Raw Score	Age 6	Age 7	Age 8	Age 9	Age 10+	Raw Score
40					99	40
39				99	98	39
38		99	99	96.5	95.5	38
37	99	98	95	89	88	37
36	97	94	86	78	75	36
35	89	87	74	64	59.5	35
34	81	78	62	49.5	46	34
33	74	69	50	37	34	33
32	63	58	39	26	24	32
31	53	46	30	18.5	16	31
30	47	35	23	14	11	30
29	38	27	17	10	6	29
28	31	21	12	7	3	28
27	23	17	9	5.5	2	27
26	15	14	6	4	1.5	26
25	11	11	5	3	1	25
24	9	9	4	2.5		24
23	8	7	3	2		23
22	7	6	2	1		22
21	5	4	1.5			21
20	4	3.5	1			20
19	3	2.5				19
18	2	1.5				18
17	1	1				17

Table 2
Arbitrary Aptitude Levels Expressed As Percentile Ranks

High ....80—99%
High Average ....60—79%
Average ....41—59%
Low Average ....21—40%
Low ....1—20%

Table 3
IMMA Tonal Aptitude Levels For Different Age Groups Based On Raw Scores

Aptitude	Age 6	Age 7	Age 8	Age 9	Age 10+
High	34 or above	35 or above	36 or above	37 or above	37 or above
High Average	32-33	33-34	34-35	35-36	36
Average	30-31	31-32	33	34	34-35
Low Average	27-29	28-30	30-32	32-33	32-33
Low	26 or below	27 or below	29 or below	31 or below	31 or below

Table 4
Tonal IMMA Means and Standard Deviations

Age	N	Mean	SD
6	88	29.9	4.26
7	268	30.6	4.44
8	344	32.3	3.76
9	367	33.3	3.79
10, 11, 12	412	33.9	3.02

CHAPTER FOUR
Sound-Before-Sight-Before-Theory

Truth never dies, but it lives a wretched life.

—Yiddish proverb

The idea that music teachers should teach sound before sight before theory is an old one. It certainly did not begin with Edwin Gordon. As far as I know, it's rooted in the general learning theories of Johann Heinrich Pestalozzi[4]; and during the nineteenth century, Lowell Mason (1838) wrote music curriculum guidelines for the Boston schools based on the following Pestalozzian ideas:

1. Teach sound before sign.
2. Lead the student to observe by hearing and imitating instead of explaining.
3. Teach but one thing at a time—rhythm, melody, and expression—before the child is called to attend to all at once.
4. Require mastery of one step before progressing to the next.

---

4 Although the hierarchy sound-before-sight-before-theory comes from Pestalozzi, the concept of *structured* sound—that is, sound organized syntactically—is Gordon's contribution.

5. Give principles and theory after practice.[5]

These five guidelines give rise to the following comprehensive hierarchy: In order for children to receive optimal music instruction, they need to develop audiation skill, the ability to sing in tune, and the ability to move in a coordinated manner; they also need to build a vocabulary of tonal and rhythm patterns through audiation and performance; these basic skills—audiation and performance ability— enable children to learn to read and write music notation with comprehension; and *these* skills, in turn, enable children to learn music theory.

This sequence, so fundamental to Music Learning Theory, is probably old news to you. Still, there are a few issues that you may find troubling.

First, why do I limit the "sound" part of sound-before-sight-before-theory to the tonal and rhythm dimensions of music? You may think that I'm ignoring other dimensions of musical "sound" such as style, dynamics, and timbre. Certainly these should be taught, but their elements need not be sequenced in learning hierarchies. One need not, for instance, expose children to Baroque music before Classical music, *forte* before *mezzo forte*, or the timbre of woodwind instruments before the timbre of brass instruments.

Second, how do students learn to read and write music notation? Specifically, how do children take information *from* the page, and then bring understanding *to* the page? For that matter, how do they cope with the fact that the notation they are learning does not precisely represent the music they can already audiate? I'll talk about these issues in greater detail in chapter 10.

Third, how do students learn music notation apart from music theory? According to the Pestalozzian hierarchy, children should learn to read and write music notation *before* they learn music theory. But how do teachers separate the two? What *is* music theory anyhow?

---

5   Although Mason does not expressly say so in his fifth curriculum guideline, I take the word "practice" to mean specific musical skills such as listening, performing, reading, and writing.

Music theory is music that exists only in theory; that is, it doesn't exist at all. For music to be real, it must exist either acoustically or audiationally. For example, if I hear the seventh degree of a dominant seventh chord resolve downward by step to the third degree of a tonic chord, I'm hearing real music. If I hear the music in my mind—and I understand what I'm hearing—then I'm audiating real music. But if I merely *talk* about dominant sevenths, scale degrees, and stepwise movement, then the music I'm talking about doesn't exist in reality; it doesn't even exist as sound in my mind; it exists only in theory.

Let me bring up one more thing about the hierarchy sound-before-sight-before-theory that may strike you as odd. In chapter 3, I was discussing individual differences among children; now I'm talking about universal sameness—a hierarchy that applies to everyone. Isn't this a contradiction? Actually, I don't see it as contradictory or paradoxical. It's simply something that music teachers must come to terms with: Each child is unique, but in some ways, as this hierarchy makes clear, all children learn the same way.

In fact, this hierarchy is not only universal but also irrefutable. No other ordering of the components "sound," "sight," and "theory" would form a logical music learning hierarchy. Music is, after all, an aural art; a logical hierarchy must, therefore, be ordered in a way that is consistent with the nature of the subject.

I've heard arguments from colleagues who insist that, since some children have poor auditory discrimination skills, those children should be taught to understand music visually rather than aurally. Mysteriously, these colleagues almost always begin their argument by talking about mathematics: Some students might learn multiplication tables visually, they say, while others might learn them by setting them to a rhyming chant; others might make cardboard cutouts of numbers and learn through tactile associations. Since children can use many different "learning styles" to learn mathematics successfully, shouldn't they have the same freedom when they learn music?

Before I argue against that point of view, let me say that this teaching approach is sometimes called "modality matching" (Wepman, 1964). The idea behind it is that children should learn a subject through whatever physical sense is most natural for them. Now certainly that makes sense and I believe it's logical up to a point. I can see its value for such subjects as mathematics, science, and social studies. But it loses its value when teachers apply it to music, art, typing, cooking, and driver education. Why? Because, with those subjects, children must develop a specific sense *in order to learn them.*

For example, suppose a student learning to touch-type had poor tactile abilities. Could she simply learn to touch-type by developing a different sense? Could she learn to type by *staring* at the typewriter? By *listening* to the clicks of the keys? Perhaps I'm pressing this point a bit too hard. The thrust of my argument is simply this: It's counter-productive to bypass a student's poorly developed tactile sense (or aural sense, in the case of music) when the development of that sense is an integral part of the subject she's learning.

Can children learn music through a multisensory approach— that is, through their aural and visual senses simultaneously? Eventually yes; initially no. To learn music, students must develop, as Dean (1989, p. 348) puts it, "independence of the ear from the eye." But they would never develop this independence if both senses were being used at the same time, one always as a crutch for the other. Certainly, once children develop their aural and performance skills sufficiently, and once they learn to read music, their reading and listening skills will reinforce each other, just as they do in language. But audiation skill, as Walters fancifully put it, is the "jump-starter" of the whole process.

To sum up: In spite of modality matching, learning styles, and multisensory approaches, the basic hierarchy of sound-before-sight-before-theory still stands.

Perhaps you're still skeptical about this. Can *any* skill learning hierarchy be broad enough to serve all children? Impossible! you say. But consider this: all children who learn to run, have learned to stand

and walk first. There is simply no exception. Standing-before-walking-before-running is a universal skill learning sequence. Such a learning sequence in music may not be so far-fetched after all.

CHAPTER FIVE
Tonal Syntax

*"Take care of the sense,
and the sounds will take care of themselves."*

—Lewis Carroll,
Alice In Wonderland

I mentioned in the last chapter that the "sound" part of sound-before-sight-before-theory refers specifically to the tonal and rhythm dimensions of music. Specifically, how do children audiate tonal and rhythm content? Do they audiate isolated pitches and isolated durations, or groups of pitches and groups of durations? If they audiate groups of pitches, do they audiate intervals, or do they audiate patterns with specific functions such as tonic major? If they audiate groups of durations, then how do students keep track of all the rhythmic complexities in music? These are tough questions. I will do my best to answer them in the next two chapters. In this chapter, I will focus on the tonal dimension of music.

During a lecture on tonal intervals[6], Leonard Bernstein (1992) said:

> One simple note by itself is not music—not even a molecule of music, not even an atom. A single note is more like a single proton or an electron, which, as you know, are

---

6 This lecture, entitled *Musical Atoms: A Study of Intervals*, was first delivered in 1965 as part of the Young People's Concert Series.

meaningless all by themselves. You need at least one of each—at least two atomic particles— in order to create an atom. And in exactly the same way you need at least two notes before you can begin to have an atom of music. . . But once you have two notes, you suddenly feel a relationship between them, like an electrical tension. There is already the beginning of musical meaning (pp. 255-256).

If Bernstein is correct, then the children-audiate-one-note-at-a-time theory is out. Still, we're left with this question: do children audiate intervals, or patterns with specific functions? One of the basic tenets of Music Learning Theory is that *children do not audiate intervals; they audiate functional tonal patterns made of intervals.*

Let me go into this in some detail. During the 1970s, Gordon studied the difficulty levels of audiated patterns; and he discovered, among other things, that a tonal pattern can be easy to audiate, moderately difficult to audiate, or very difficult to audiate depending on its context. For example, patterns A and B in Figure 5-1 are descending major thirds beginning and ending on the same pitches. Nevertheless, pattern A is moderately difficult to audiate; pattern B is easy to audiate (Gordon, 1989).

Pattern A   Pattern B

FIGURE 5-1

You'd think that, since both patterns are identical, they would have the same audiation difficulty level. Since they have *different* audiation difficulty levels, it follows that we audiate them differently. But how could it be that we audiate patterns A and B differently when they sound exactly the same?

Here's the catch: The children that Edwin Gordon tested—and incidentally, he tested over *eighteen thousand children* from all over the country—heard Pattern A in the context of major tonality, and they heard Pattern B in the context of minor tonality. Notice that all other aspects of these two patterns are the same: the pitches, the interval, even the harmonic function. The only variable is the tonal context. It follows, then, that the tonal context these patterns were placed in determined their audiation difficulty levels. In other words, the tonal context of the patterns determined how children audiated them. What other explanation can there be? In short, we don't audiate pitches, or even intervals; we audiate *structured* pitches, pitches that we organize into patterns that relate to a tonal center. Or to use fancy linguistic terminology, we don't audiate musical phonology (sound), but musical *syntax* (structured sound).

Perhaps you don't yet see the relevance of all this. Gordon, you may think, sits alone in an ivory tower calculating standard deviations and correlation coefficients while the rest of us go on with our lives. Nothing could be further from the truth. The fact that we audiate syntactically is, perhaps, the most sensational discovery ever made in the history of music education! It renders all traditional music curricula—those that emphasize the teaching of pitch matching, melodic contour, intervals, and scales—obsolete.

What's wrong with teaching pitch matching? Nothing, provided you *first establish tonality* so that the student who is to match the pitch is aware of its tonal context. Asking a child to sing a pitch—even a *series* of pitches—out of context is like asking a man in a lifeboat, adrift at sea, to find the mainland without a compass. It makes no sense to play a series of notes on the piano for a child and then ask her to "pick them out of the air." Pitch matching, in and of itself, is a pointless activity; but asking a child to audiate and sing a resting tone after you've established tonality—now *that's* meaningful. Syntax, syntax, syntax! Go to sleep tonight with that word on your lips.

What's wrong with teaching melodic contour? Nothing I suppose, provided your students have reached a fairly sophisticated level of tonal audiation. But melodic contour has no meaning for a child who is just beginning to learn to audiate. How does it help a student to audiate a melody if she learns that the melody first goes up, and then goes down, and then goes up again? And what do words like "up" and "down" and "high" and "low" mean to a seven-year-old music student? Nothing, unless you show her notation; and if you do that, you will inevitably teach audiation and notation at the same time. A horrendous teaching procedure.

"High" and "low" *seem* to be easy concepts for children to grasp. Visually, they *are* easy concepts. But, as I pointed out in the last chapter, although music can be represented visually, it is not a visual art; it is an aural art. Therefore, in music, "high" and "low" are not even descriptions; they are nothing but *metaphors*—easy, perhaps, for adults to understand. But what's easy for adults to understand is not necessarily easy for children. My experience is that most children cannot grasp the meaning of these adult metaphors without notation. And certainly they mean nothing to an out-of-tune singer. (How much luck have you had correcting out-of-tune singers by telling them to "sing just a little bit higher" or "sing a smidgen lower"?) Once again, it makes sense to teach "high" and "low" only *after* you have taught children to audiate and to perform tonal patterns in specific tonalities with specific harmonic functions.

But, you may argue, children need to understand "high" and "low" in order to read music. I disagree. Ask yourself with total frankness: How much success have you had teaching students to read notation with the following pieces of advice? "When one pitch sounds higher than another, it will appear higher on the staff; when one pitch sounds lower than another, it will appear lower on the staff." But how much higher, and how much lower? Clearly this teaching technique is seriously flawed. For instance, how would such a vague explanation of "high" and "low" help children to read examples A and B in Figure 5-2? How would it help children even to tell them apart?

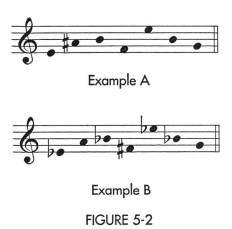

Example A

Example B

FIGURE 5-2

What about intervals? Some colleagues I've spoken to tell me that, without their knowledge of the sounds of intervals, they'd be lost. They need to know the sounds of intervals in order to sing complex vocal music. In fact, some of the best vocal sight readers I know have a thorough knowledge of intervals. Certainly, this knowledge is important; but if a musician knows *only* intervals and not pattern functions, she will be extremely limited as a thinking musician. Why? Because, even though a rose is a rose is a rose, a perfect fourth is not a perfect fourth is not a perfect fourth. A perfect fourth can be a cadential pattern, a subdominant pattern, a dominant pattern, and so on. Before we teach intervals, we must first teach patterns in specific tonal contexts so that, later on, intervals will mean something to students. Once again, syntax reigns supreme.

And scales? Let them be the *last* things you teach. Keep in mind that tonalities existed before scales. No one ever said to a composer, "Here's the dorian scale. Go write 'Scarborough Fair.'" Composers wrote music in various tonalities, and then *theorists* came along and put the characteristic pitches of those pieces in scale order. The moral is clear: Teach children to audiate tonalities by teaching songs and patterns; save scales for later.

I can imagine my colleagues in Philadelphia reading this and finding it distressing. Let me emphasize that nothing in our tonal curriculum is "wrong." All we need to do is change the *order* of certain things and make sure that we teach syntax before phonology, notation, and theory. Unfortunately, many music teachers begin by teaching phonological aspects of music—pitches, intervals, melodic contour—and neglect almost completely the teaching of tonal syntax.

How does one teach tonal syntax? Briefly, there are two ways. A teacher may establish tonality and then teach patterns by rote. Or, at a more advanced level, a teacher may sing a "chain" of patterns and then teach the tonality of that "chain." I'll have more to say about this in Part Two of this book.

Let me conclude this chapter with yet another quote from Leonard Bernstein. Regarding the sense of tonality, Bernstein (1966, p. 12) writes:

> The sense of tonality—the sense of a tonal magnetic center with subsidiary tonal relationships—is built into the human organism; we cannot hear two isolated tones, even devoid of any context, without immediately imputing a tonal meaning to them. We may differ from one another in the tonal meaning we infer, but we infer it nonetheless. . . . And the moment a composer tries to abstract musical tones by denying them their tonal implications, he has left the world of communication.

CHAPTER SIX
Rhythm Syntax

*". . . and she told two friends, and they told two friends,
and so on, and so on, and so on. . ."*

—Slogan from a television commercial featuring
Fabergé Organic Shampoo

If Edwin Gordon's tonal theories confuse many people, his rhythm theories baffle many more. I'm not quite sure why. It could be that his ideas about rhythm are rooted in movement, and some musicians are uncomfortable moving rhythmically; they would much rather *read* rhythm notation or *theorize* about it. To audiate rhythm and to engage in smooth, flowing, continuous movement is, well, embarrassing. Gordon's rhythm theories might be difficult to understand for another reason: when most people think of rhythm, they usually don't think of continuous movement; they think of counting beats. True, beats are an important part of rhythm. But one of the first things I teach my students is that beats mean nothing to a person who cannot move with a relaxed, artistic sense of flow.

The main problems with Philadelphia's rhythm curriculum are: 1) it is too beat-oriented; 2) it has us teach note values such as quarter notes and eighth notes *before* rhythmic patterns with specific beat functions; and 3) it was written under the assumption that meter comes from accenting certain beats. Let me discuss these points one at a time.

What's wrong with being beat-oriented? Nothing, provided your students can first move in a coordinated manner. If they can't, then they will have a poor sense of tempo as they perform rhythm patterns. Why? Because they will not be able to feel the space *between* beats.

Imagine this: You're driving on a highway, route something-or-other; you're not quite sure of the number. You don't know how close you are to your destination or to the nearest rest stop. All you know is that your car keeps moving with you in it. And the ever-changing scenery holds your attention. Still, there's that nagging question: Where am I? Suddenly you see a sign—NEXT REST STOP 10 MILES. You begin to relax. Just then, up comes another sign—ROUTE 27 NORTH. Aha! So *that's* where you are. Another sign—ROUTE 39 EXIT 2 MILES. Another one—NEXT REST STOP 5 MILES. Soon another one—NEXT REST STOP 3 MILES. Before long—NEXT REST STOP 1 MILE. How comforting these signs are! Without them, you'd be lost on a highway with pretty scenery.

Music is like that. It constantly moves forward in time like your car on the highway. And how do you tell where you are in the music? What are the musical equivalents of the roadsigns? Beats, of course. Specifically, melodic rhythm with its many beat functions. That's why it's so important to teach children how beats function in music. But it's not enough that we teach students to "keep the beat." First we should teach them to move as the music moves—continuously.

What is the mysterious relationship between beats and continuous flow? Gordon has come up with a theory of rhythm that goes a long way in answering that question. He believes that rhythm is made up of three fundamental elements: macro beats, micro beats, and melodic rhythm.[7] You may be thinking, "Oh no. More 'Gordonisms'

---

7 Some people think of macro beats as long beats and micro beats as short beats. I prefer to think of them as "large" beats and "small" beats. The terms "long" and "short" carry with them the suggestion of articulation—of legato and staccato—which has nothing to do with macro and micro beats. Why, you may be asking, did Gordon coin these words in the first place? Aren't the terms "large" and "small" good enough? No. Macro beats and micro beats are proper names; the words "large" and "small" are not proper names but merely descriptions. Eventually children will be taught to *name*— not merely describe—the beat functions they can perform.

to deal with." Actually they're very easy to understand. Let me begin by explaining what macro beats are.

Try an experiment: Listen to a metronome ticking steadily. Tick. . . tick. . . tick . . . tick. . . tick. . . tick. . . tick. . . tick. Every "tick" is the same. Now choose one "tick" over the others; that is, pretend that one of those "ticks" is stronger or more prominent than all the others that preceded it. (It really won't be stronger, but just humor me.)

Now what do you hear? I'll bet that you don't just hear one strong "tick" and lots of weak "ticks"; instead, you probably hear this: *strong* . . . weak. . . *strong* . . . weak. . . *strong* . . . weak. . . *strong* . . . weak. Am I right? Of course I am, but how can this be? After all, all the metronome beats are the same. Yes, true, objectively. But your brain does not process the metronome beats objectively. You are subjectively pairing beats in spite of what the metronome is actually doing. Pairing beats—that's the key. These paired beats are called macro beats.

How do we help children to feel these beats? The progression is this: first, we should encourage our students to move continuously; then, as they're moving continuously, we should encourage them to shift their body weight and move back and forth or side to side; in this way they will "discover," through movement, their own physical symmetry; eventually they will relate their body's symmetrical design to symmetry in music, to the pairing of beats, rhythm patterns, and phrases.

Perhaps you're skeptical about symmetry as a readiness for understanding macro beats. On the subject of symmetry, Leonard Bernstein (1966) wrote:

> All music [has] one great factor in common: symmetry, that precise balance that derives from the physical biformity of the human being. This biformity creates in us a biological need, which then becomes an aesthetic demand (p. 98).

Just think of the human heart. It's pulse is not just 1, 1, 1, 1. There are two phases to each heartbeat, expansion and contraction, 1-2, 1-2 (p. 91).

[Even] a waltz, whose greatest claim to fame is that it's in three-quarter time, turns out to be just as much a slave to dupleness as anything else. A waltz is a dance, and a dance is performed on two legs. It's not 1-2-3, 1-2-3 but *left*-2-3, *right*-2-3. *The meter may be triple, but in a larger rhythmic sense a waltz is every bit as duple as a march* [Italics supplied] (p. 97).

What is Bernstein saying? Because of our physical symmetry, our built-in "dupleness," we pair . . . everything. Regardless of meter, every phrase of music—every beat of music—is half of a larger whole. We understand rhythm (and musical form as well) to the extent that we anticipate a consequence from an antecedent.

Notice that when Bernstein talks about the meter of a waltz, he talks about two kinds of beats occurring together. One beat is the left. . . right. . . left. . . right. . . left. . . right. . . left. . . right kind; the other is the 1-2-3-1-2-3-1-2-3-1-2-3 kind. Put them together and you have *left*-2-3, *right*-2-3, *left*-2-3, *right*-2-3. The left . . . right. . . left. . . right. . . beats are the macro beats. But what are the smaller 1-2-3-1-2-3-1-2-3-1-2-3 beats called? You guessed it! They're called micro beats.

But, you may be asking, why must we teach macro and micro beats at all? What's wrong with simply teaching half notes, whole notes, and quarter notes? The fact is that your students don't audiate isolated durations such as half notes and whole notes; they audiate rhythm patterns with specific functions. It isn't enough to teach a series of eighth notes such as those in Figure 6-1.

Keep in mind that we audiate syntactically rather than phonologically. In other words, the "sound" of a series of eighth notes is far less important than the context that the eighth notes are placed in.

Certainly your students would not audiate the four eighth notes in Figure 6-1 the same way in patterns A, B, C, or D.

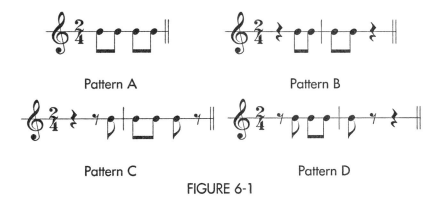

Pattern A   Pattern B

Pattern C   Pattern D

FIGURE 6-1

These four eighth notes may *sound* the same regardless of the context they're placed in, but in each new context they take on a different *feel*. What makes a particular beat feel a certain way? Its rhythmic function, of course. Is it a macro beat? A micro beat? A division of a micro beat? An anacrusis?

How ridiculous it is for teachers to hold up a mathematical "rhythm chart" and teach a series of whole notes, then a series of half notes, then a series of quarter notes, eighth notes, sixteenth notes—and then stop. ("Just remember this, boys and girls: Two of *these* notes equal one of *these*.") This phonological approach to teaching rhythm reminds me of the joke about the man who says, "The only book I ever bother to read is the dictionary. I figure it's got all the other books in it."

What's wrong with teaching that meter is created by a series of accents? Brace yourself for what I'm about to tell you: Accents have nothing to do with meter. There. I said it. Let me say it again. Accents have nothing to do with meter! You don't believe me, do you?

Try this: With your left hand, patsch a series of big steady beats. Use your whole arm and make your arm go up high before it comes down on the beat. Those are the macro beats. Got it? Good.

Now tap triple micro beats with your right hand at the same time. Notice what's happening. A macro beat coincides with every *third* micro beat. Right?

Okay, now do this: stop your left hand completely, but keep the right hand moving to triple micro beats. Try *not* to accent any beat over the others. Do you notice something peculiar about those triple micro beats? They're not triple micro beats anymore! They have become macro beats, albeit *small* macro beats.

Now start moving your left hand to macro beats again. Ah, that's better. Triple meter is restored, and the smaller beats in your right hand make sense once more.

What does this say about meter? Do we create meter by accenting one beat over other beats at regular intervals, or by dividing larger beats into smaller ones? Do we start with macro beats and then divide them? Or do we start with micro beats and then elongate them? Who knows? Who cares? The point is that we understand meter in music when we understand how macro beats and micro beats *work together*.

You can discover this for yourself: listen to any piece of music with a consistent tempo; start moving to the macro and micro beats; you'll discover that the meter of the music is revealed when you audiate and perform two different beat functions—macro beats and micro beats—simultaneously.[8]

One last piece of advice: Don't ask what 6/8 means.

I hear this all the time. When music teachers talk to me about Gordon's work, they invariably talk about the time signature 6/8. Is 6/8 duple or triple? Again, my advice is: don't ask. Or rather, ask; but prepare yourself for an answer you may not like. If you say that the time signature 6/8 means compound duple meter, I have some news for you. There is no such thing as a time signature. And 6/8 means nothing. No, I have *not* gone mad! Let me explain.

---

8 Certainly you can create a metrical context by tapping rhythm patterns with one hand and, with the same hand, accenting every macro beat. But what you're doing is compensating for the fact that one hand is doing the work of two.

A "time signature" such as 6/8 is not a time signature because it tells a musician nothing about time or tempo. Also, it's not a meter signature because it tells nothing about meter; or rather, it tells nothing about any one meter in particular. (Gordon calls it a "measure" signature, for lack of a better name.) Think about the many meters and rhythm patterns that can be notated in 6/8. In Figures 6-2, 6-3, and 6-4, you'll see just a few.

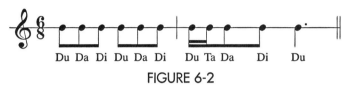

Du Da Di Du Da Di   Du Ta Da   Di   Du

FIGURE 6-2

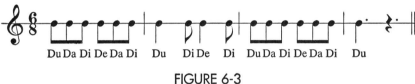

Du Da Di De Da Di   Du   Di De   Di   Du Da Di De Da Di   Du

FIGURE 6-3

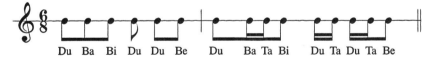

Du Ba Bi Du Du Be   Du   Ba Ta Bi   Du Ta Du Ta Be

FIGURE 6-4

Underneath the music, you'll see some strange nonsense syllables. Actually they're not nonsense syllables but rhythm solfège syllables. I'll talk more about them in the second part of this book. All you need to know right now is that "Du" corresponds to the macro beat.

Let's say that the eighth-note pulse in Figure 6-2 equals 140 beats per minute. Clearly these patterns are in triple meter.

But what about the patterns in Figure 6-3? Let's say that the *dotted-quarter-note* pulse equals 140 beats per minute. Quite a different situation, isn't it? The tempo is now so fast that the patterns cannot possibly be in triple meter. Instead of two macro beats per measure, there is now only one macro beat per measure. The patterns are in duple meter with underlying triplets. Chant them for yourself and you'll see what I mean.

And what about those quirky patterns in Figure 6-4? They are in an unusual meter that Gordon calls "unpaired intact" meter. Unusual? Unpaired? Intact? Quite a mouthful!

Gordon calls any meter "unusual" when the macro beats are not of equal temporal length. Think about it: In duple and triple meters, the macro beats are all equal. Not in Figure 6-4, however. Both measures have three macro beats in them; each macro beat is quite different from the others.

Three macro beats? Wait a minute. Aren't macro beats supposed to come in pairs? Yes. According to Gordon, even in unusual meters, macro beats are paired; and when one macro beat is left over, as in the case of a group of three, that "extra" macro beat goes unpaired—supposedly. Frankly, this "unpaired" business leaves me cold. After all, aren't the three macro beats in the first measure of Figure 6-4 paired with the three macro beats in the second measure? Sure they are. My advice is: take Gordon's "unpaired" term with a grain of salt. Remember Bernstein: everything is, in a broad sense, duple; everything is paired; we cannot escape our physical symmetry.

Take one last look at the patterns in Figure 6-4. Do you see the eighth note all by itself in the first measure? What in the world is that? A macro beat? A micro beat? My guess is that it's both! In this context, that duration serves two functions; and (this is the strange part) it does not divide into micro beats; it divides into division beats. Bizarre. How Gordon came up with the term "intact" to label this kind of beat, I'll never know. But any series of patterns that has an intact macro/micro beat is in "intact" meter.

Finally, those two measures in Figure 6-4 are in—are you sitting down?—*unusual unpaired intact meter.*

Amazing, isn't it? The measure signature 6/8 is, as Gordon puts it, "enrhythmic." That is, it can mean many different meters:

duple, triple, unpaired intact. And don't forget the meters I haven't mentioned. You can use 6/8 to notate patterns in "combined" meter, in which you have a combination of duplets and triplets that frequently alternate; you can string together *all* the examples I've written and create a series of patterns that Gordon would call "multi-metric."

I guess what I'm trying to say is, don't start out by asking what a particular measure signature "means." In fact, don't start with notation; instead, start with real music. Make up a series of patterns in any meter and then ask, "How many different ways can I notate this?" You may surprise yourself!

Certainly, don't waste your time asking what 6/8 is. Don't find yourself shouting, "GORDON SAID THAT 6/8 IS TRIPLE, BUT MY THEORY TEACHER TOLD ME IT'S DUPLE!" 6/8 is neither triple nor duple. 6/8 is nothing. . .until you decide it's something.

Let me conclude this chapter by saying that rhythm is an elusive subject. Perhaps no one will ever understand it fully. I certainly don't understand it as thoroughly as I'd like to. All I can tell you is, given my limited understanding, I've learned to cope with the complexities of rhythm in a particular way. Instead of counting beats, I feel them; instead of theorizing, I move.

CHAPTER SEVEN
Music Education on Four Levels

I will make your descendants as numerous
as the stars of heaven and the sands on the seashore.

—Genesis 22:17

It's time to take a deep breath. Prepare yourself. This is a long and complex chapter. In it, I tie together many of the important ideas from the previous chapters. I hope you have read them carefully, because now we are ready, at last, to explore the question: What makes Music Learning Theory tick? Perhaps a good way for me to begin answering that question is to say, flat out, that there is no "Gordon Method." In fact, the terms "Gordon Method" and "Gordon System" are misleading for two reasons.

First, Music Learning Theory is not the sole property of Edwin Gordon. It's a series of ideas that belong to every music teacher and musical thinker. Gordon may be the person most associated with Music Learning Theory; but he has a long line of distinguished predecessors from such disparate disciplines as linguistics, psycholinguistics, general learning theory, and psychology.

Second, Music Learning Theory cannot be the "Gordon Method" because it's not a method to begin with. One of the important themes of this book is that Music Learning Theory gives rise to, perhaps, tens of thousands of methods without being a method itself. How can this be? Recall what I said in the introduction to this book, that music education could be separated into four topics. They are: 1) the musical and pedagogical principles that give rise to Music Learning Theory, which I will refer to from here on as "irrefutable truths about music and music education"; 2) Music Learning Theory itself; 3) learning methods; and 4) teaching techniques. Now try to think of these topics in a hierarchy. You can see them as levels of a pyramid in Figure 7-1.

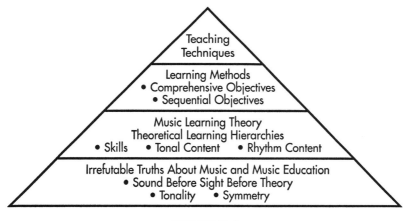

FIGURE 7-1

Don't let this pyramid scare you! It's really quite easy to understand. Let me explain the contents of this pyramid in detail.

Irrefutable Truths About Music and Music Education

At the base of the pyramid, there are the three universal truths about music and about music education that I discussed in chapters 4, 5, and 6. Briefly, they are:

1. Children should develop audiation skill, the ability to sing in tune, and the ability to move in a coordinated manner; they should also build a vocabulary of tonal and rhythm patterns through audia-

tion and performance; these skills enable children to learn to read and write music notation with comprehension; and *these* skills, in turn, enable children to learn music theory.

2. Children understand the tonal dimension of music when they learn to organize pitches into tonal patterns that relate to a tonal center.

3. Children understand the rhythm dimension of music when they become aware, through movement, of their own physical symmetry, and begin to relate that symmetry to reiterated beats, rhythm patterns, and phrases.

Music Learning Theory

At the next level, there is Music Learning Theory. It's made up of three parts: a sequence for learning musical *skills*, a sequence for learning *tonal content*, and a sequence for learning *rhythm content*.[9] And where do these learning hierarchies come from? The three "irrefutable truths," naturally. Let me emphasize that, although Gordon's three learning hierarchies follow closely on the heels of the "irrefutable truths," they are still, for all their complexity and sophistication, just theories. I will now discuss Gordon's learning sequences one at a time.

The tonal learning sequence is based on the notion that tonality is basic to the human species. In Gordon's opinion, children *in this culture* should learn tonal patterns in major and minor tonalities before they learn patterns in other tonalities such as dorian and phrygian. Also, students should be taught to audiate and to perform tonic and dominant patterns in major and minor tonalities before they are taught to audiate more complex pattern functions.

Gordon bases his rhythm learning sequence on the notion that human beings organize rhythm by pairing beats, rhythm patterns, and

---

9 As I said in the introduction, musical *skills* refer to specific abilities such as music reading, creating, singing, etc. *Content* refers to specific aspects of the music, such as its melodic rhythm, its harmonic functions, etc.

phrases. In his opinion, children *in this culture* should learn patterns in duple and triple meters before they learn patterns in unusual meters. Also, students should be taught to audiate and to perform macro and micro beat patterns before they are taught more complex rhythm patterns.[10]

All in all, Gordon's tonal and rhythm learning sequences have few surprises in them. It's the *skill* learning sequence that usually throws people. Here is a basic introduction to it.

The skill learning sequence is nothing more than an expansion and refinement of the Pestalozzian hierarchy sound-before-sight-before-theory. In the next few paragraphs, I'll explain how Gordon *expanded* the hierarchy; later, in chapter 10, I'll explain how he *refined* it. Gordon expanded Pestalozzi's three-part hierarchy into the following eight steps:

Step 1: Students build a vocabulary of tonal and rhythm patterns by listening, singing, chanting, and moving.

Step 2: Students sing and chant the same tonal and rhythm patterns they learned during Step 1, but with tonal and rhythm solfège. They use solfège syllables as tools to help them understand pattern functions. For example, students are taught that, when they hear a pattern with the syllables *do, mi, and so* in any combination, they are hearing a tonic major pattern.[11] Clearly, without solfège, it would be impossible for most students to learn pattern functions.

---

10 Teachers should certainly expose children to a wide variety of tonalities and meters and not limit themselves to major and minor, duple and triple. Gordon's tonal and rhythm hierarchies refer to those moments of classroom teaching devoted to pattern instruction.

11 One question I often hear is: Aren't tonics and dominants examples of music theory? No. Keep in mind that music theory is music that doesn't exist in reality. As long as you and your students *audiate and sing* tonic and dominant patterns—and not merely *talk* about them—you'll be teaching those harmonic functions in reality, not in theory.

Step 3: Students recognize the tonality and meter of various *series* of familiar patterns.

Step 4: Students read and write familiar patterns with the aid of solfège.

Step 5: Students read and write tonal and rhythm patterns in a series and with an understanding of the tonality and meter of each series.

Step 6: Students generalize information about unfamiliar music based on previous learning. Here are some examples of generalization tasks: students identify whether two unfamiliar patterns are the same or different; students name the functions, the tonality, or the meter of unfamiliar patterns with the aid of solfège; students read unfamiliar patterns or write them from dictation.

Step 7: Students create, improvise, and compose music with or without the aid of solfège.

Step 8: Students learn theoretical information, such as the letter names of lines and spaces on the staff, the names of intervals, the various halfsteps and wholesteps in scales, the time value names of notes, the nature of the circle of fifths, and so on.

Of the eight steps, the first five belong to a generic category that Gordon calls "discrimination learning." The emphasis is on the teacher imparting information. The last three steps belong to another generic category that Gordon calls "inference learning." The emphasis is on the student teaching herself.

I mentioned in the introduction to this book that Music Learning Theory will probably change in response to new insights. How might this eight-step learning sequence change? In general, it will grow rather than diminish in complexity. No level of learning in

Gordon's skill learning sequence is expendable;[12] and no two steps (certainly no two steps of discrimination learning) should be interchanged. The sequence simply lacks the precision that future music learning theorists will give it. Frankly, I believe that, even though it grew out of Pestalozzi's unshakable hierarchy, Gordon's skill learning sequence is destined to remain a theory no matter how complex and sophisticated it becomes. Still, Music Learning Theory is stable enough to give us the tools we need to design our curriculum.

Why do we need Music Learning Theory? Because the "truths" at the base of my pyramid are too broad, too vague to be used to design a curriculum. Music Learning Theory is the link, the liaison between universal truths that apply to all children, and the learning method we will eventually write for our students only.

Learning Methods

This brings me to the next level of music education: Learning methods made up of specific sequential and comprehensive objectives. Here are some examples of sequential and comprehensive objectives from my tonal curriculum. (I want to emphasize that these are just *possible* objectives. I'm sure that better ones can be devised.) As you read them, you'll notice that the comprehensive objectives—the units—are fairly general, whereas the sequential objectives are highly specific. Notice also that the objectives are cumulative: when students complete six or seven sequential objectives, they have completed one unit; and each unit gives students the readinesses to complete the next unit.

Here are the first six units:

Unit 1—Students will sing, with a neutral syllable, tonic and dominant patterns in major and minor tonalities.

---

12 Perhaps step 5, which Gordon calls composite synthesis, is expendable. More about this in chapter 10.

Unit 2—Students will name, and sing with solfège syllables, the same major patterns taught in Unit 1.

Unit 3—Students will create (with a neutral syllable) and improvise (with tonal syllables) tonic and dominant patterns in major tonality.

Unit 4—Students will name, and sing with solfège syllables, the same minor patterns taught in Unit 1.

Unit 5—Students will create (with a neutral syllable) and improvise (with tonal syllables) tonic and dominant patterns in minor tonality.

Unit 6—Students will recognize different *series* of tonic and dominant patterns as being in major or minor tonality.

I won't burden you with a complete series of sequential objectives for achieving all six units. But I do think it's important for you to read the sequential objectives for completing the first three:

Unit 1

Comprehensive Objective: Students will sing, with a neutral syllable, tonic and dominant patterns in major and minor tonalities.

• The student sings the resting tone of patterns in major tonality. (The patterns the teacher sings must be dominant major, then tonic major ending on the resting tone.)

• The student sings the resting tone of patterns in minor tonality. (The patterns the teacher sings must be dominant minor, then tonic minor ending on the resting tone.)

• The student sings tonic major patterns.

• The student sings dominant major patterns.

• The student sings tonic minor patterns.

• The student sings dominant minor patterns.

Unit 2

Comprehensive Objective: Students will name, and sing with solfège syllables, the same major patterns taught in Unit 1.

• The student sings the resting tone in major tonality *(do)*. (The patterns the teacher sings must be dominant major, then tonic major ending on the resting tone.)

• The student recognizes patterns with the syllables *do, mi,* and *so* as tonic major patterns.

• The student recognizes patterns with the syllables *ti, re, fa,* and *so* as dominant major patterns.

• The student discriminates between tonic major patterns and dominant major patterns.

• The student sings tonic major patterns.

• The student sings dominant major patterns.

Unit 3

Comprehensive Objective: Students will create (with a neutral syllable) and improvise (with tonal syllables) tonic and dominant patterns in major tonality.

- The student creates *any* pattern in response to a tonic major pattern.

- The student creates *any* pattern in response to a dominant major pattern.

- The student improvises one tonic major pattern in response to a tonic major pattern sung by the teacher.

- The student improvises one dominant major pattern in response to a dominant major pattern sung by the teacher.

Differences between Music Learning Theory and Learning Methods

According to Gordon (1993), there are three important differences between Music Learning Theory and a learning method with specific objectives.

1. The main difference has to do with flexibility. Perhaps you believe, after reading my objectives, that methods based on Music Learning Theory are so fixed that they become stifling. Actually, they can be as flexible as you want them to be.

For instance, notice that my comprehensive objectives do not coincide exactly with the eight-step learning sequence that I listed a few pages back. I have children *sing* patterns, then *name* patterns, then *create and improvise* patterns. According to Gordon's eight-step learning sequence, I should have students *sing* patterns, then *name* patterns, *then combine them in a series.* Creativity and improvisation should come later. Have I broken the rules? Not at all. Look back at Gordon's eight steps. I've simply made a *temporary skip* from rote learning (steps 1 and 2) to creativity and improvisation (step 7), and back to rote learning again. Perfectly legal. (I'll explain more about how to do that in Part Three of this book.)

Let me give you another example to show you the flexibility of methods that can grow out of learning theory. Suppose that your students are having trouble learning to read notation. Possibly they need more aural training, or they need to review solfège syllables. So you, responding to their need, move them back to the skill level they need to review.

What does all this mean? It means that your learning method can be flexible in two ways: 1) You can review skills and content that you taught earlier, or 2) you can skip children ahead, temporarily, to a level of inference learning. In theory, learning should proceed sequentially; but real life doesn't work that way. There is, after all, a difference between Music Learning *Theory* and music learning *reality*.

2. One of the basic tenets of Music Learning Theory is that children learn musical content most effectively when they are taught one new bit of content at a time. Still, we should make sure that we don't dwell too long on any one tonality or meter. If, for instance, we teach our students patterns in major tonality for three months, then we should also expose them to patterns in minor tonality during that time. The logic behind this is that children who are taught to audiate only one tonality or only one meter, do not really learn to audiate *any* tonality or meter; **making comparisons, knowing what something is *not* contributes to knowing what it is.**

Look closely at my sequential objectives. You'll notice that the content changes frequently from major to minor, from tonics to dominants.

3. In theory, musical skills and content are sequenced in separate hierarchies. ("Sound before sight before theory" is separate from "major and minor before dorian and mixolydian.") In reality, we must combine skills and content. How could we teach our students tonic major patterns, for instance, without giving them something to do with that content. Will they *read* tonic patterns? *Write* tonic patterns?

Sing tonic patterns with tonal solfège? *Create* tonic patterns? *Theorize* about tonic patterns? And in what *order* will they do these things? To quote Walters: "Skills and content are as interdependent as a lock and key."

I should mention at this point that, although we will naturally combine the tonal and rhythm dimensions of music during traditional classroom activities, we should *separate* them during pattern instruction; that is, we should teach tonal patterns devoid of melodic rhythm and rhythm patterns devoid of pitch. The rationale for this can be understood with the following example: children who hear two patterns, such as those in Figure 7-2, will insist that they're hearing *two different tonal patterns,* even though the patterns are different in melodic rhythm only.

FIGURE 7-2

To avoid this confusion, teachers should chant rhythm patterns such as those in Figure 7-3 with vocal inflection but not with specific pitches.

FIGURE 7-3

Also, teachers should sing the pitches in a tonal pattern with a consistent tempo, but with as little reference as possible to any meter as in Figure 7-4.

FIGURE 7-4

Perhaps you find this upsetting; perhaps you believe that it's downright unmusical to sing tonal patterns devoid of rhythm. Keep in mind that tonal patterns will be meaningful if you present them in a specific tonal context, and if you teach them as part of the whole-part-whole learning process. But what about musical aesthetics? What about expression? All I can tell you is that children will learn to audiate the tonal dimension of music much more thoroughly and with greater sureness if, during pattern instruction, they are taught tonal patterns devoid of melodic rhythm; and the better they understand the tonal dimension of music, the better they can appreciate music. I'll have more to say about this in the next chapter.

Teaching Techniques

There are techniques for teaching rote songs and traditional classroom activities, and most music teachers are well acquainted with those. On the other hand, there are techniques for teaching tonal and rhythm patterns, and most teachers don't have a clue about those. I'll provide detailed suggestions for teaching patterns in Part Three of this book.

Teachers have enormous flexibility when they choose teaching techniques. Ironically many teachers, even many of those who understand Music Learning Theory, fail to take advantage of this. They believe, wrongly, that there is one "right way" to teach patterns, one "right way" to establish tonality, one "right way" to coordinate rote songs with pattern instruction.

Look back, for a moment, at the four levels of my pyramid. You may notice that from the base of the pyramid to the top, teachers have more and more options available to them. For example, it's easy for teachers to throw out many of Gordon's teaching techniques and invent their own. (I do this often myself.) It's more difficult for them to criticize the sequential and comprehensive objectives found in *Jump Right In: The Music Curriculum*, Gordon's K-8 general music series. And it's more difficult, still, to refute aspects of Gordon's theoretical hierarchies. (In chapter 10, I challenge many of his ideas about how children learn to read and write music notation most effectively.) But the "irrefutable truths," as my name for them suggests, are beyond reproof.

Summary

Although Music Learning Theory is an outgrowth of universal educational truths, it will always remain a theory. The nature of Music Learning Theory is that *one cannot use it directly*; to use it, a music teacher must design a method based on it, and then come up with teaching techniques to get the method off the ground.

Since there's no one right way to design a method based on Music Learning Theory, a music curriculum may take one of many possible forms. In fact there are, perhaps, tens-of-thousands (!) of possible methods that can grow out of it. One can, for instance, write a music curriculum that combines Music Learning Theory with Orff and Kodály activities.[13]

Finally, think of Music Learning Theory as a "theme" that may give rise to thousands of possible "variations." The first edition of *Jump Right In: The Music Curriculum* is one variation; the second edition of *Jump Right In* is another; *Jump Right In: The Instrumental*

---

13 It's a red-herring to argue that Orff and Kodály methodologies are "just as good" as Gordon Learning Theory. The fact is that Orff, Kodály, and Gordon have provided music teachers with different things. Orff and Kodály gave music teachers wonderful activities and teaching techniques; Gordon has provided music teachers with theories of how children learn music based on his experimental and observational research. It's silly and pointless to haggle over whose contributions are the most valuable. We need to understand the work of *all three* music educational theorists; and for that matter, we also need to understand the insights of other

Series is a third; mine is a fourth. And so it goes. If we in the Philadelphia School System were to collectively design our own curriculum based on Music Learning Theory, that would be a fifth.

Frankly, I can't think of a more exciting prospect for our future.

giants in music education such as Dalcroze, Suzuki, and Laban.

Having said that, however, I should point out that the basic argument of this chapter—indeed, of this book—is that *any* music curriculum we write must be based on Music Learning Theory, regardless of what other forces help to shape it. For more detailed information about combining Music Learning Theory with other methodologies, please see D. L. Walters and C. C. Taggart (Eds.), *Readings in Music Learning Theory.* 1989. Chicago: G.I.A.

CHAPTER EIGHT
The Myth of Musical Insensitivity

There are more things in heaven and earth, Horatio,
Than are dreamt of in your philosophy.

—William Shakespeare,
Hamlet

The belief that Music Learning Theory leads to unmusicality is an accusation aimed not at learning theory, but at its supporters; and unfortunately some of Edwin Gordon's critics have resorted to making it. For example, while comparing the ideas of Edwin Gordon to those of Bennett Reimer, Richard Colwell and Frank Abrahams (1991) wrote:

> Reimer, but not Gordon, willingly accepts. . .how tonal events arouse tendencies, cause expectations, and produce various kinds and degrees of resolutions and satisfactions. Whether audiation is a step toward perceiving this tension and response, toward regarding music as *an expressive form* [italics supplied] rather than as a symbol, is doubtful. . . .
>
> In suggesting that *learning theories cannot provide the structure for the learning process* [italics supplied], Reimer suggests that psychology can be applied to anything from music to housecleaning, but psychology cannot differentiate

between the teaching of cooking and the teaching of music. That is, it cannot provide the answer of what should be taught to all students and what, within the subject (music), should be chosen to be taught—only philosophy can do that because these are questions of value (p. 34).

What is one to make of this barely coherent passage? I doubt that Gordon would agree that audiation is, indeed, "a step toward regarding music as a symbol rather than an expressive form." Frankly, what *is* a "symbol" in contrast to an "expressive form"? And what about the mind-numbing assertion that learning theories cannot provide the structure for the learning process? In fact, that's exactly what they do!

What I find most disturbing about the contents of their article is that Colwell and Abrahams attempt to draw a distinction between music philosophers and music psychologists, as though a music educational thinker had to be one or the other. Colwell and Abrahams then become self-appointed music philosophers and relegate Gordon to the psychologist (i.e. the inferior) camp. Their "philosophical" stance seems to me to be based on this shallow syllogism: 1) Gordon is a music psychologist; 2) No music psychologist can decide what music students should learn ("because these are questions of value"); 3) Gordon (and by extension, supporters of Music Learning Theory) cannot decide what music students should learn.

Colwell and Abrahams even go so far as to call Gordon a behaviorist, implying that he denies the importance, possibly the existence, of affective, emotional responses to music.[14] It's true that Gordon rarely writes about the role of affect in music education, but that does not mean that he denies its importance or its existence. To quote Carl Sagan: "Absence of evidence is not evidence of absence."

How do we music teachers and music pedagogical thinkers rise

---

14 Gordon's (1991, p. 65) response to being called a behaviorist is as follows: "Quite frankly, and regardless of what others may believe, I consider myself to be more in line with cognitive and developmental thinking than with behavioral principles."

above labeling and mud-slinging? One constructive approach might be for us to draw a distinction between musical *meaning* and musical *expression*. Leonard Bernstein (1976), who was certainly one of the most emotionally demonstrative conductors of the century, had this to say about musical meaning:

> Music has intrinsic meanings of its own, which are not to be confused with specific feelings or moods, and certainly not with pictorial impressions or stories (p. 131).
>
> A piece of music is a constant metamorphosis of given material, involving such transformational operations as inversion, augmentation, retrograde, diminution, modulation, the opposition of consonance and dissonance, the various forms of imitation (such as canon and fugue), the varieties of rhythm and meter, harmonic progressions, coloristic and dynamic changes, plus the infinite interrelations of all these with one another. These *are* the meanings of music (p. 153). [Italics his]

Ultimately, music teachers are responsible for teaching their students the meanings of music—and nothing else. Of course, teachers should encourage students to react emotionally to music; and of course, teachers should *not dis*courage students from doing so; and certainly, teachers should show, with sincerity and without embarrassment, their own emotional reactions to music. Such modeling for students is a crucial part of quality music education.

But modeling emotional responses, and telling students what and how to feel are two different things. Unfortunately, teachers who set out to teach "music appreciation" often foist their own feelings and opinions onto students. "Does this chord convey a feeling of tension or relaxation? Does it make you feel happy or sad?" The student is praised if she dutifully answers that a dominant chord conveys tension, a tonic chord conveys relaxation, a major triad sounds happy, a minor triad sounds sad.

Innocent, well-intended questions they are; *but they contribute nothing to an understanding of musical meaning,* and they may cause students who have other opinions to feel inadequate! Why burden your students with such unproductive (possibly *counter*productive) questions when there is a whole universe of musical meaning for them to explore? It is to that exploration of musical meaning that I now turn.

Part Two

Curriculum Reform

CHAPTER NINE
Informal Guidance

Your children are not your children.
They are the sons and the daughters of Life's
longing for itself.
They come through you but not from you,
And though they are with you yet they belong not to you.
You may give them your love but not your thoughts,
For they have their own thoughts.
You may house their bodies but not their souls,
For their souls dwell in the house of tomorrow,
which you cannot visit, not even in your dreams.
You may strive to be like them,
but you cannot make them just like you.

—Kahlil Gibran
The Prophet

There's a wonderful moment in the book *Loving Each Other: The Challenge of Human Relationships* (1984, p. 59), in which Leo Buscaglia writes about how children learn to speak:

All the world's children develop language in the same way. They will babble, go through an initial stage called echolalia, will proceed to words, then sentences. All they seem to need is a language-filled environment where they can hear the sounds of language. I will never forget an American lady I met while teaching in Taiwan, who stood back in awe and said, "Imagine, two-year-old children in the streets are speaking Chinese!" What did she expect they'd be speaking? Greek?

Babies are absorbent—like diapers. They have the knack for taking in everything around them without being taught a thing. In light of that, what can a music teacher teach a baby? Everything and nothing.

For the last two years, I have been teaching in a wonderful music program for children from birth to age six. It's called the Children's Music Development Program (CMDP) and it's part of Temple University's Music Preparatory Division.

The classes must be seen to be believed. They are as different as can be from the typical kindergarten or first grade music classes in the Philadelphia Public Schools. What makes them different? The CMDP curriculum is based on a single philosophical principle: a child is not a miniature adult. That's it. Let me say that again. A child is *not* a miniature adult!

One of the biggest mistakes that we make in the Philadelphia School System is that we assume that children think like adults, see the world like adults, audiate music like adults. They don't. And so our traditional instruction programs are doomed from the start. Why do we stick to the belief that first-grade children are ready for what we have to offer? Why must we teach them to keep a steady beat? To understand melodic contour? To "contrast melody alone with accompanied melody"? Here's a mind-blower: *Why must we teach them anything at all?* After all, parents don't "teach" their children to speak; parents don't "teach" their children to walk. They *guide* them; they *don't instruct* them.

Do you sense that I'm headed somewhere with all this? I hope so. Here is Gordon's suggestion to me, and my suggestion to you: Give young children informal guidance in music before you give them formal instruction.

I won't lie to you. What I'm suggesting will not be easy to carry out; that is, it will be easy for children but difficult for you. You see,

Edwin Gordon's research in this field—and it is probably the best work he has ever done—is pioneering and still quite new. If you learned how to teach music back in the 1960s and 1970s, the chances are that the contents of this chapter will startle you. You'll have to learn about music pedagogy all over again; you'll have to learn how to teach, or rather, how *not* to teach. My purpose here is to give you a head start.

In his book *A Music Learning Theory for Newborn and Young Children* (1990), Gordon asserts that there are seven stages of musical development that all children seem to go through before they develop audiation skill. Here they are, and I apologize for throwing them at you all at once:

Stages of Preparatory Audiation

Stage One: Absorption
Stage Two: Random Response
Stage Three: Purposeful Response
Stage Four: Shedding Egocentricity
Stage Five: Breaking the Code
Stage Six: Introspection
Stage Seven: Coordination

Don't worry. I intend to explain the nature of these stages one at a time in detail. Perhaps the best way for me to do this is simply to tell you what goes on during a typical music class on Saturday morning at Temple University. First I'll tell you what we do and how we do it; then I'll tell you how children are likely to respond to us.

Stage One: Absorption

Listening is the basis of all music learning. Therefore the musical environment we create for children is vitally important to their musical growth. Here are some of the details of that musical environment that we create every week.

Usually there are between seven to ten children in a class. The kids come in with their parents. Everyone flops on the floor. Sometimes everyone forms a circle. Then we start singing. We don't teach anything by rote. Instead, we simply expose children to songs, chants, patterns, and pre-recorded music.

During a typical class period, I sing roughly fifteen to twenty songs in at least four or five tonalities: major, minor, dorian, phrygian, lydian, mixolydian, and occasionally locrian. Our songs and chants are in many different meters such as duple, triple, and "unusual" meters such as 5/8 and 7/8. Our purpose is to expose children to a world of musical possibilities. As our curriculum coordinator Beth Bolton puts it: "We immerse children in an audiation bath!" Variety is the key. Although the other teachers in the program use different songs and chants from the ones I use, the *variety* of musical content from class to class, teacher to teacher, is the same.

Virtually every song we sing is without words. Let me repeat that: *We sing songs without words*. All we use are neutral syllables such as "bah" throughout a song.

This is a real shocker for a lot of people. Typically music teachers will teach songs with words, or with a story-telling text, to keep children interested and attentive. You know the sort of thing I mean: "There were ten in the bed and the little one said 'roll over'. . .There were nine in the bed. . . ." The problem is that the words in a song do not help children to grow musically. Children tend to pay more attention to the words and they ignore the intrinsic musical elements such as the tonality and the meter. Mind you, I'm not saying that the children I teach every Saturday morning *understand* the tonalities and meters of the songs that I sing. I simply expose them to many tonalities and meters by singing songs to them so that they can absorb those intrinsic musical elements.

Here is one of the songs without words that I made up for my students. One of the delights about being in this program is that I get to make up lots of songs and chants for the kids! Notice that my song is in phrygian tonality and that the meter is 1-2, 1-2, 1-2-3.

Here are a few more things you should know about the songs that we sing.

All our singing is unaccompanied. No piano, no guitar! That way, children can concentrate fully on the melody alone.

Also, we make a real effort to sing the same song always in the same key. This is weird. No one really understands why, but apparently transpositions confuse children if they have not yet emerged from tonal babble.[15] They will tend to "tune out" rather than try to cope with the confusion. If a child is used to hearing a song in E flat, then we don't change it to D.

The same thing is true for rhythm. Our songs and chants are performed each time in the same meter and, if we can, at the same tempo. Once again, children will become confused if they hear the same chant with a different tempo than what they are used to. Certainly, we *don't* change a song from major to minor tonality, or a chant from duple to triple meter!

What about our chants? Here's where we get goofy: OOOOOOOMM BAH! Choom, choom, *BAH*! Enough said.

One thing is certain: We all use lots of vocal inflection when we chant. We let our voices rise and fall a great deal. (I know that children tend to tune me out when I chant to them in a monotone.) An interesting note: it doesn't throw children off if I use different vocal inflections each time I perform a chant. In fact, it tends to captivate them.

What about the pre-recorded music? We never use "children's records" with children! We expose children to "adult" music in a variety of styles and genres. "But wait a minute!" I hear you saying. "By exposing children to 'adult' music, aren't you treating them like miniature adults?" Not at all, because we don't expect them to listen to music the way an adult would. We encourage them to move to the music, to react to it. That's all.

In Gordon's opinion—and I think he's right—children tend to respond most favorably to music with *lots of dynamic and timbre con-*

---

15 According to Gordon, people go through **musical babble** in the same way that one-year-old children go through language babble. Someone who cannot sing in tune and has no sense of tonality is still in tonal babble. Someone who cannot move with a consistent tempo and has no sense of meter is still in rhythm babble. It's a sad fact that most of the adults in our society are still in tonal babble, rhythm babble, or both. They are still toddlers musically! On the other hand, three-year-old children can emerge from tonal and rhythm babble if they are given good informal guidance in the first few years of their lives.

trasts. This suggests that Haydn symphonies, Strauss tone poems, and jazz would hold a child's attention in a way that Mozart string quartets, rock, or rap would not.

Let me say a few words about movement. We never force a child to move; and we certainly never move a child's limbs! I see parents doing this all the time in my classes, and it drives me up a wall. Parents naturally want to get their money's worth out of our program; so if they see that their child is not responding, they will move the child's body. I usually tell parents, "If she doesn't want to move, that's cool; if she does, then move *with* her, not *for* her."

The movements that we model for the children are very important. Our movements are generally relaxed, flowing, and continuous. Also, we generally use large muscle movement such as hip movement and arm movement from the shoulder. If I'm working with kindergarten and first-grade children who are still in rhythm babble, I might have them pretend that they're soaring like an eagle or that they're under water. This encourages them to feel a sense of both weight and flow.

Isn't it a curious fact that marching and clapping are so important in most preschool and kindergarten music programs? Nevertheless, they are vastly overrated. Clapping is a bad activity, mainly because it doesn't involve weight. Patching is much better, especially if the arm movement is large and starts from the shoulder. Walking is much better than marching and is particularly valuable if the children can already move in place in a *continuous, flowing manner.*

Now that you know some of the things we do in our classes, let me tell you about the responses we are likely to get from children.

Stage Two: Random Response

I honestly know very little about the typical responses of children who are at this stage of development. I do know that children will respond randomly before they respond purposefully. That is, children will make babble sounds and random movements. (I see this occasionally in the class for severely retarded children that I teach in one of my schools in Philadelphia.) The sounds have no meaning for adults and the movements are uncoordinated by adult standards. This is to be expected. All I do is encourage the children to move and make sounds and I don't worry if they are not imitating me. In fact, I'm sure that they're not even *trying* to imitate me yet.

You may have concluded from what I've written that the responses children give us at this stage are not necessarily musical. And you're right. Sometimes a child will just look at us; sometimes she'll drop her jaw and tilt her head; sometimes she'll smile; sometimes she'll burst out laughing; sometimes she'll cover her face with her hands; sometimes she'll start running around the room.

If this strikes you as an inauspicious beginning for a child's music education, you might want to keep this in mind: There is a difference between a random *action* and a random *response*. It makes sense that children will demonstrate random actions before random responses. For instance, if a child drops her jaw and stares at us for no reason, that's a random action. But if a child, who has not paid any attention to us before, suddenly drops her jaw and stares at us after we chant a rhythm pattern, that's a random response.

Stage Three: Purposeful Response

At the next stage of development, children will respond musically to what we do, but in ways that we cannot predict. I get this all the time from my kindergarten students. I sing one thing to a child; she sings something else. And the pleased look on her face tells me that she doesn't know, or even *care*, that what she sang was different from what I sang.

The teachers at CMDP all have different personal teaching styles, as you would expect, but still, there are some things that we have in common. First we encourage children to sing and chant *alone*. Group singing is kept to a minimum. Second, along with songs and chants and pre-recorded music, children are exposed to tonal and rhythm *patterns* at this stage. Third, and perhaps most important, we don't worry that the children aren't imitating us; we encourage the children to respond to the patterns anyway they want to.

Let me talk about the patterns we teach for just a moment.

We always establish duple or triple meter with a chant or two before we perform rhythm patterns in duple or triple meter. Similarly, we always establish major or minor tonality with a song or two before we sing patterns in major or minor tonality. ***Songs and chants first; patterns second***. We follow this sequence for two reasons: First, this approach is in keeping with the whole-part-whole learning process. And second, even though children are not audiating syntax at this point, we try to guide them in that direction by singing and chanting patterns with structural meaning.

We're very careful to keep the tonalities, keys, tempos, and meters of the patterns consistent with the tonalities, keys, tempos, and meters of the songs and chants. For example, we don't chant triple meter patterns after performing a chant in duple meter. Also, we don't sing patterns in e minor after performing a song in d minor.

The patterns themselves have some important characteristics as well. I'll talk about the rhythm patterns first, the tonal patterns second.

The rhythm patterns we chant at this stage have two underlying macro beats in them. Also, we tend to put complex melodic rhythm only on the *first* macro beat. In Figure 9-1, you'll see some examples of the rhythm patterns we might chant at this stage.

The tonal patterns we sing are three-note, stepwise, diatonic patterns in major and minor tonalities such as those in Figure 9-2.

FIGURE 9-1

FIGURE 9-2

The way we sing the tonal patterns is interesting. We sing them rather quickly, on one breath, and in a legato style. Even though we don't expect the children to imitate us yet, their responses often will be close to what we're doing. At this stage, they're *exploring* their singing voices; and the stepwise patterns encourage them to do that.

Notice my choice of keys in Figure 9-2. The tonal patterns do not have to be sung in D major or d minor; but keep this in mind: a child's initial singing voice range is from D (above middle C) to the A (a perfect fifth above). When children sing below a D, they might sing with a speaking voice quality; when children sing above an A, at B flat or B natural just below high C, they go through a voice break. In short, if your songs and patterns are above or below that five-note range—D above middle C, to A, a perfect fifth above—you will force the children into a soprano-screech register or an alto-growl register. So, before I sing stepwise, diatonic patterns, I make sure to establish tonality with songs that have a tonic of D, E flat, or occasionally E.

During a performance of a song, we naturally combine tonal and rhythm elements. But during pattern instruction—as you might by now predict—we sing the tonal patterns without melodic rhythm. And we chant the rhythm patterns without pitch but with lots of vocal inflection.

Typically, children won't respond to patterns until they've heard many songs and chants. And if they do respond by singing, chanting, or moving, they won't do it to try to imitate us. The fact is, they're not interested in what we're doing; they're interested only in what *they're* doing. We never—and I cannot say this often enough—we *never* criticize them when they sing or chant differently from us. The fact that they're singing or chanting at all is a miracle.

Important: *If a child responds in any way, we try to imitate her.* This is one of the hallmarks of our program. It's the opposite of what you would normally find in a typical music program in which children are expected to imitate the teacher right from the start. In our program, *we* do the imitating! I don't fully understand the psychology behind it, but children often take comfort in the fact that an adult has tried to imitate them; it gives them the impetus to try to imitate others. In a manner of speaking, to imitate a child is to hold a mirror up to that child.

Stage Four: Shedding Egocentricity

Eventually, children will realize (and you can see this by the quizzical look on their faces) that what they just sang or chanted was different from what you just sang or chanted. They still can't imitate you with precision, but now they're aware of their limitations. Many children find this intensely frustrating; they want to imitate you but they can't. To help them, we follow the same procedure that we used when the children were at stage three (and, of course, we work one-on-one): we sing or chant a pattern; we listen to the child's response; we imitate what she did; and then we see if she can imitate us. If she can, then she's really imitating herself with our help.

As I said earlier, we first expose children to rhythm patterns with only two strong beats, and to tonal patterns with pitches that move diatonically by step. Typically the children won't be able to imitate us. But they will often respond by spontaneously singing the resting tone or, more often than not, the dominant note, sometimes called the "reciting" tone. Or, if they're responding to our rhythm patterns, they might patsch or chant micro beats. These are indications that they have moved into stage four and are ready for more complex tonal and rhythm patterns.

Stage four is characterized by three things: 1) Children give us an "audiation stare" as if to say, "What are *you* doing?" 2) We chant patterns with four underlying macro beats instead of two. 3) We sing tonal patterns that are arpeggioed rather than stepwise.

The "audiation stare" is a fascinating event. It's one of the most important moments in the life of a music student, and one of the most thrilling moments in the life of a music teacher. We sing something; the child sings something else; and then she looks at us like we're from Mars. What makes this so exciting? The child is beginning to discriminate something from something else. It's the first sign that she is moving into the world of audiation. She doesn't know what's wrong, but she knows *something's* wrong. The frustrating thing is that we cannot teach a child to move to the next stage and "break the code," that is, imitate us with precision. She must do this on her own. But the patterns we perform, and the way we perform them can help.

The rhythm patterns consist of four underlying macro beats such as the patterns in Figure 9-3. I find it interesting that the rhythm patterns are not only symmetrical; they *emphasize* symmetry. Notice that the melodic rhythm is rather complex on the third underlying macro beat; that is, the third macro beat is qualitatively different from the first two, suggesting that the first two macro beats are paired; by default, the next two macro beats are also paired. If the complex melodic rhythm were to fall on any other beat, the symmetrical nature of the patterns would not be as obvious.

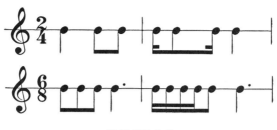

FIGURE 9-3

The tonal patterns that we sing at this stage are cadential patterns (*so-do* ascending and descending in major tonality, and *mi-la* ascending and descending in minor tonality, sung without solfège of course). Earlier, at stage three, when children responded to stepwise patterns, they had no understanding of the tonal functions of those patterns; at this stage, when children try to imitate cadential patterns (or better still, perform them on their own) they are beginning to understand tonal syntax. More profoundly, they are beginning to understand that a phonological phenomenon—the proximity of the root to the fifth in the overtone series—can take on structural meaning. Naturally they can't verbalize all this. Just one look says it all.

When we perform cadential patterns—and later, arpeggioed patterns—we sing them in a non-legato style. That is, we put a smidgen of space between pitches.

The tonal patterns are in major and minor tonalities as you might expect, but our choice of keys is unusual. We try to make sure not to exceed a child's initial singing voice range (D to A). Therefore, before we sing ascending or descending fifths at this stage, we establish tonality with songs in D or occasionally E flat; before we sing ascending or descending fourths, we establish tonality with songs in G, A flat, or A.

Stage Five: Breaking the Code

Once children can imitate these patterns with reasonable precision, we have them imitate three-note tonic and dominant patterns. This, of course, does not happen overnight. Children will imitate us with some precision one week, and then sing out of tune or chant out of tempo the next. *Patience* is the operative word.

Eventually they will imitate us nearly perfectly every time they sing or chant. What does this mean? Have they. . . arrived? Are children ready for formal instruction once they can imitate tonal and rhythm patterns with precision? No. There's still something missing. Recall what I said in chapter 1: a musician who audiates must internalize music and not merely imitate it or memorize it. Imitation—even *perfect* imitation—is shallow and fleeting.

Stage Six: Introspection

At this stage, the essential difference between imitation and audiation becomes critical—and tricky. In order for children to move beyond mere imitation, they must develop the ability to listen to themselves, critically assess their own performance, and make corrections in rhythm and intonation. I've seen this many times in my classes. A child in my class has just chanted a rhythm pattern accurately, or perhaps she has just sung a tonal pattern with good intonation. To me, it sounded fine. To her, it was a disaster. The look on her face says, "Wait a minute! That's not what I meant to do. Let me try it again."

How does a teacher help a child to critically assess her own performance, and to understand that there is a difference between what she performed and what she *meant* to perform? No one knows. Perhaps there's nothing a teacher can do; that is, perhaps this sort of realization is purely self-generated and is not something that one can teach. Teachers may not even be able to *guide* students at this stage. I suspect I'm being overly pessimistic here. The fact is that this is the trickiest stage of musical development. *No one* knows very much about it. All I can do is tell you what I do know.

There is a mysterious relationship between breath and thought. We breathe, of course, without thinking; but our thoughts may affect the *way* we breathe. Consider this: somehow, we automatically know what size breath to take when we express our thoughts in casual converation. It's a chicken-or-egg question: Do our thoughts impel us to breathe with a certain force and at a certain tempo? Or does our breathing trigger our thoughts? In either case, the relationship between our breathing and our thinking extends to our audiation. **We cannot audiate unless we breathe.**

But how do we encourage our students to breathe? Offhand, this seems like a ridiculous question, but it's really a serious one. We breathe all the time; but sometimes our breathing helps us audiate and sometimes it doesn't. How do children coordinate their breathing with their thinking and audiating? Answer: Through continuous, relaxed movement. For strange as it sounds, children breathe and audiate when they are relaxed; and if we encourage them to *move gracefully*, they will breathe naturally and they won't feel like they "have to breathe." We encourage them to move when they're listening to music, when they're singing patterns, when they're chanting rhythms.

Important: We encourage children to move continuously— *never rhythmically*—as they're singing tonal patterns. But we do encourage them to move rhythmically as they're chanting rhythm patterns. Eventually children will be able to do three things at the same time: patsch micro beats, chant rhythm patterns, and move their upper body continuously.

So then. Movement triggers breathing, and breathing triggers audiation. But how? I wish I knew. All I can tell you is that the relationship between breathing and audiating is built on a quirky, mystical phenomenon: No moment in music is complete in itself. Think about it. Every moment in music has preceding and succeeding moments. The comedian George Carlin tells a joke along these lines:

"I feel a moment coming up. It's. . .wait. . .it's still in the future. It's almost here. Getting closer. . . Closer. . .Here it comes. . .And. . .HERE IT IS, and. . .Aw, it's gone, man." So it is with music. I could get fancy and refer to the before-, during-, and after-time in music as the anacrusis, the crusis, and the metacrusis; but I think the ideas are easy to understand without those words. The point is this: Children who imitate and don't audiate have no sense of "before" and "after." All they know is "during." When they perform music, they don't prepare for it or respond to it; they just do it.

On the other hand, the "good confusion" that children experience at stage six—the look that says, "Let me try that again."—is a sign that children are moving beyond imitation and are becoming artistically independent.

Stage Seven: Coordination

At stage seven, children can coordinate their breathing and movement with their singing and chanting. Children no longer feel uncertain about their performances; in other words, they can correct their own rhythm and intonation *before they perform.*

Since stage seven coincides with formal instruction, I should end this chapter right now and begin the next one. But before I do that, I want to bring up one more point: How does a teacher tell if a child is audiating or merely imitating? Externally, there *is* no way to tell. After all, a child may imitate perfectly and still not audiate.

And even if a teacher *can* tell if a child is audiating, what difference does it make? If we can get our students to imitate us with perfect intonation and rhythm, who needs audiation?

A devastating question! It's as much a *moral* question as a musical one. And it brings me right back to our main problem which I stated in my introduction: We are not educating our students to become independent musicians and independent musical thinkers. Where does this independence come from? Audiation, of course. So now, our problem can be restated and shortened: We music educators are not teaching our students to audiate. Period.

Why not? Because we expend so much time and energy teaching our students to imitate. And why do we do this? So that we can get kids up on stage to perform. We and our students can then be "visible." That's the obsession of many music teachers I've talked to. "We must be *visible*," they insist, "so that we can make parents and administrators happy; that way, we can keep our jobs."

Let's assume there's a grain of truth to the idea that we must be "visible." I'm still repulsed by this line of thought for two reasons.

First of all, there are better ways, nobler and less vulgar ways, to be visible. Why don't we—to make a frankly revolutionary statement—simply tell parents and administrators exactly what we teach and how we teach it?

Second, and perhaps more important, our way of being visible—banging the music on the piano, drilling it into kids' heads, putting them up on stage, and encouraging them to imitate—makes a mockery out of the art of music. The problem is *not* the fact that we put on shows. On-stage, public performances are a crucial part of music education. The problem is the *way we prepare* for these shows. Performance must serve education; not the other way around!

My advice is this: Let's teach our students to strive not for perfect imitation, but for imperfect audiation. Why imperfect? Because a musician who audiates the music she performs is never satisfied with her performance. There is always "something wrong"—audiationally, technically—with the phrasing, dynamic choices, articulation, intonation, or rhythmic accuracy. Perhaps only the musician herself is aware that there's a problem. A music student who imitates has no such problems; her perfect imitation leads to perfect satisfaction. By contrast, the mark of any true musician, of any serious artist, is *dis*satisfaction—and a life of thrilling and unending artistic growth.

CHAPTER TEN
Formal Instruction

*The universe belongs to those who,
at least to some degree, have figured it out.*

—Carl Sagan
Broca's Brain

O nce all that preparatory audiation stuff is out of the way, children are ready to begin formal instruction in music. Tonics, dominants, macro beats, micro beats—the whole bit.

In chapter 7, I told you about Edwin Gordon's eight-step, skill learning sequence. I told you that it was an expansion of Pestalozzi's three-step sequence, sound-before-sight-before-theory. Here are Gordon's eight steps again:

Step 1: Students build a vocabulary of tonal and rhythm patterns by listening, singing, chanting, and moving.

Step 2: Students sing and chant the same tonal and rhythm patterns they learned during Step 1, but with tonal and rhythm solfège.

Step 3: Students recognize the tonality and meter of various *series* of familiar patterns.

Step 4: Students read and write familiar tonal and rhythm patterns with the aid of solfége.

Step 5: Students read and write tonal and rhythm patterns in a series and with an understanding of the tonality and meter of each series.

Step 6: Students generalize information about unfamiliar music based on previous learning.

Step 7: Students create, improvise, and compose music with or without the aid of solfège.

Step 8: Students learn theoretical information, such as the letter names of lines and spaces on the staff, the names of intervals, the various halfsteps and wholesteps in scales, the time value names of notes, the nature of the circle of fifths, and so on.

Back in chapter 7, I promised you that I'd explain how Gordon *refined* this sequence. Well, here we go.

GORDON'S SKILL LEARNING SEQUENCE

Discrimination Learning
AURAL/ORAL
VERBAL ASSOCIATION
PARTIAL SYNTHESIS
SYMBOLIC ASSOCIATION
Reading—Writing
COMPOSITE SYNTHESIS
Reading—Writing

Inference Learning
GENERALIZATION
Aural/Oral—Verbal—Symbolic (Reading and Writing)
CREATIVITY/IMPROVISATION
Aural/Oral—Symbolic (Reading and Writing)
THEORETICAL UNDERSTANDING
Aural/Oral—Verbal—Symbolic (Reading and Writing)

One way that Gordon refined these eight steps was by giving them fancy, scary names. First I'll give you the names of the eight levels of learning; then I'll explain, in detail, the nature of each level individually. (As you read this hierarchy, keep in mind that the most basic skill level is on the top of the list, and the most difficult skill level is on the bottom.)

To be honest with you, the first time I read this hierarchy and tried to make sense out of it, I got nowhere. All I got was the worst headache I can remember. My goal in this chapter is to take you through the hierarchy painlessly.

Step One: Aural/Oral

In order for children to understand music, they must build a vocabulary of tonal and rhythm patterns, comparable to a vocabulary of words in language. The trouble is that music learning is different from language learning. Children build a language vocabulary by associating words with things that they see, hear, touch, taste and smell. On the other hand, children build a music vocabulary by hearing patterns, then singing or chanting them—*and then naming them.* What accounts for that extra step in music? Bernstein (1976), once again, seems to have the answer:

Language leads a double life; it has a communicative function *and* an aesthetic function. Music has an aesthetic function only. For that reason, musical surface structure is not equatable with linguistic surface structure. In other words, a prose sentence may or may not be part of a work of art. But with music there is no such either-or; a phrase of music is a phrase of art. It may be good or bad art, lofty or pop art, or even commercial art, but it can never be prose in the sense of a weather report. . . . To put it as clearly as possible, there is no musical equivalent for the sentence I am now speaking (p. 79).

The basic difference between music and language, according to Bernstein, is that music has no communicative function. Since language has literal meaning, children can learn, for instance, what a chair looks like and the fact that it's called "chair" at the same time. But if children sing the pattern in Figure 10-1 with a neutral syllable such as "bah," they're not naming it; they're simply performing it. It makes sense therefore, that pattern instruction is accomplished in two separate steps. First children listen to and perform, let's say, tonic major patterns; then they name them as "tonic major."

Figure 10-1

Gordon calls the first skill level, during which children merely hear and perform, the aural/oral level. He calls the second level, during which children *name* what they can perform, the verbal association level.

At the aural/oral level, children simply hear patterns and echo them in a call-and-response format. Actually it's not that simple. Teachers must make sure—and I know you've heard me say this many times—to *establish tonality or meter* before teaching patterns. Otherwise pattern instruction will be nothing but a pointless waste of time.

Before I discuss the next skill level, I should tell you that **these eight levels of learning apply to traditional classroom activities and not only to pattern instruction.** Recall that pattern instruction is the "part" of the whole-part-whole learning process. Students may learn at the aural/oral level even when they're not learning patterns. Here are some examples of what I mean. Suppose your students have learned to sing the resting tone in minor tonality as part of their pattern instruction. They can now learn to audiate and sing the resting tone of a familiar rote song in minor tonality. Another example: suppose that your students have learned, during pattern instruction, to perform macro and micro beats in triple meter. They can now learn to perform those "beat functions" at the same time they're performing familiar songs and chants in triple meter.

So it is important to keep in mind that although the examples in the rest of this chapter focus on pattern instruction, Gordon's skill learning sequence applies not only to patterns, but to full works of music and to music instruction in general.

Step Two: Verbal Association

In her autobiography, Helen Keller (1902) describes how she discovered language through tactile associations:

> [My teacher] brought me my hat and I knew I was going out into the warm sunshine. This thought, if a wordless sensation may be called a thought, made me hop and skip with pleasure.
>
> We walked down the path to the well house, attracted by the fragrance of the honeysuckle with which it was covered. Some one was drawing water and my teacher placed my hand under the spout. As the cool stream gushed over one hand she spelled into the other the word *water*, first slowly, then rapidly. I stood still, my whole attention fixed upon the motion of her fingers. Suddenly I felt a misty consciousness as of something forgotten—a thrill of returning thought; and somehow the mystery of language was revealed to me.
>
> I knew then that "w-a-t-e-r" meant the wonderful cool something that was flowing over my hand. That living word awakened my soul, gave it light, hope, joy, set it free! There were barriers still, it is true, but barriers that could in time be swept away.

I left the well house eager to learn. Everything had a name and each name gave birth to a new thought (p. 22-23).

Isn't that marvelous? The message is clear: unless we name, we cannot generate new thoughts!

Certainly children should learn to name the tonalities, meters, harmonic functions, and rhythmic functions of the patterns they have learned to perform. But how do they do this? After all, music has no communicative function. On the face of it, there's no way to tell what the patterns are. Are they tonics or dominants? In major or minor? Are they duple micro beats or triple micro beats? How can children name them if they cannot keep track of which patterns are which? The patterns simply don't "speak for themselves."

Clearly children need some kind of tool, something *outside of music* to help them; they need a way of associating those many patterns with. . .something. But what kind of associational tool is most appropriate? Certainly not tactile or kinesthetic associations. Imagine how impractical it would be to associate hundreds of different body movements with all the many tonal and rhythm patterns there are.

Verbal associations seem to be our best bet. In a musical context, verbal association means solfège. Fortunately, or perhaps unfortunately, we music teachers have verbal associations galore! Here are just some of the many solfège systems we have.

Rhythm systems include: 1) eurhythmic words, 2) mnemonic words, 3) 1-e-and-a syllables, 4) Kodály syllables, and 5) beat-function syllables.

Tonal systems include: 1) interval-names, 2) numbers, 3) fixed-*do*, 4) movable-*do* with a *do*-based minor, and 5) movable-*do* with a *la*-based minor.

Which tonal and rhythm systems should we use? Are some better than others? Should we avoid some altogether? These questions are a source of considerable debate among music teachers.

Frankly, I believe that such debates are pointless and that we could easily circumvent them. Here's what I mean. Our goal is to teach audiation; and we audiate syntactically; so *any* system we use must emphasize syntax. In other words, it must be based not on sound, but on *structured* sound. Well then. Which of the ten systems are based on musical syntax (structured sound), and which are not? The ones that *are*, we should keep; the ones that are *not*, we should throw out. Simple.

The only tonal syllable system based on syntax is **the movable-*do* system with a *la*-based minor**. The only rhythm syllable system based on syntax is the **beat-function system**. All the others are based on phonology, notation, and theory. Therefore, we shouldn't use them. "WHAT?!" I hear some of you screaming. "How can you make such a dogmatic statement? After all, I've been using the *do*-based minor system and the Kodály system for thirty years to help my students understand music."

Perhaps you believe that the choice of a syllable system is a matter of preference or personal opinion. Actually the two audiational systems—movable-*do* with a *la*-based minor, and beat-function syllables—are so integral a part of the skill learning sequence that they are more than optional teaching techniques. You might want to look back for a moment at the pyramid in chapter 7. On what level of the pyramid do these syllable systems belong? It may surprise you to learn that they belong close to the base of the pyramid on level two, not on level four at the top. The teaching techniques at level four are optional, and a teacher's success with them depends on her personal teaching style. By contrast, tonal and rhythm syllables are not optional but indispensable. It's not enough to say that the two systems I've mentioned help children to achieve at the verbal association level; those two systems *are* the verbal association level.

Let me explain why we shouldn't use the other systems if we intend to teach audiation.

I'll start with the rhythm systems.

Teachers who use the eurhythmic-word system use words, and actions associated with those words, to teach note values: walk. . . . .walk. . . . .walk. . . . .walk. . . . .run-run-run-run-run-run-run-run. . .

.gal-lop-ing-gal-lop-ing-gal-lop-ing-gal-lop-ing. The word "walk" is associated with quarter notes. The word "run" is associated with eighth notes. The word "galloping" is associated with triplets. And so on. Children walk, run, gallop, roll on the ground, march, skip, and in general, have a good time. These activities are terrific for young children; but they make lousy associational tools, mainly because there are hundreds of rhythm patterns for which there is no physical action. For instance, there's no action that goes with the patterns in Figure 10-2.

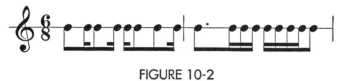

FIGURE 10-2

The mnemonic-word system has even more problems than the eurhythmic-word system. Mississippi. Is it **MIS**-sissippi as in Figure 10-3A, or missis-**SI**-ppi as in Figure 10-3B?

Pattern A   Pattern B

FIGURE 10-3

The mnemonic-word system is like the eurhythmic-word system in that there is no way to cope with complex rhythm patterns such as syncopations; another problem is that the words used are often inconsistent with the beat functions of the patterns. Is the first syllable of a word an upbeat? A downbeat? Often it's hard to tell.

The Ways Children Learn Music

The 1-e-and-a system is a beat-function system up to a point. Consider the patterns in Figure 10-4.

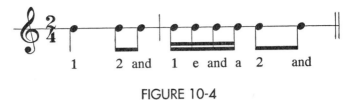

FIGURE 10-4

The numbers consistently correspond to the macro beats. Very good. The numbers, together with the "ands," consistently correspond to the micro beats. Also very good. To that limited extent, the 1-e-and-a system has internal logic. But beyond that, the system has at least three problems.

First, the syllables are awkward and difficult to say. I've heard them used with pattern A in Figure 10-5, but never with pattern B. And *certainly* never with pattern C.

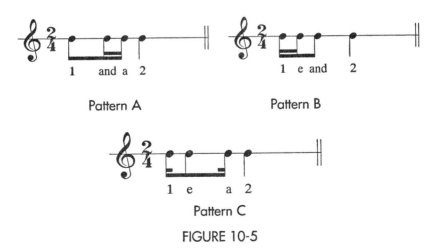

FIGURE 10-5

Another problem with the 1-e-and-a system is that the syllables for duple meter are often used for triple meter as in Figure 10-6.

Imagine how confusing it must be for a child to hear the same syllables for two different sounding patterns.

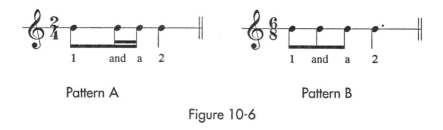

Pattern A   Pattern B

Figure 10-6

The third problem with the 1-e-and-a system is that there are no consistent syllables for triple meter. For instance, assume that both patterns in Figure 10-7 sound the same. Specifically, the quarter notes in pattern A equal the eighth notes in pattern B. Both equal, say, 70 beats per minute. Often music teachers will use 1-2-3-1-2-3 and 1-and-a-2-and-a interchangeably, even though both patterns are audiated the same way.

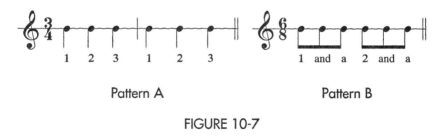

Pattern A   Pattern B

FIGURE 10-7

The Kodály system has similar limitations. Quarter notes are called *ta*, two eighth notes are called *ti ti*, and four sixteenth notes are called *ti ri ti ri*. The trouble with this approach is that the syllables serve notation and not audiation. For example, assume that Set A and Set B in Figure 10-8 sound the same. Specifically, the quarter note in Set A equals the half note in Set B.

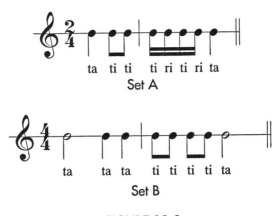

FIGURE 10-8

Take a moment to perform the patterns in Figure 10-8. Chances are that you feel the macro beats in Set A as quarter notes, and the macro beats in Set B as half notes. And yet you audiate both sets the same way! Both are in duple meter; both have the same rhythmic functions—the same macro beats, micro beats, and divisions—in the same order. The notational differences are not all that important to your audiation. And yet they *are* important with the Kodály system.

The fact is that macro beats are not necessarily quarter notes or half notes. They can be notated as a series of quarter notes, half notes, eighth notes, whole notes, double-whole notes, dotted-half notes, and so on. Their specific time value is irrelevant; all that's relevant is their temporal consistency.

The problem with all these systems is that they are inconsistent with how we audiate. Since we audiate the *functions* of beats and not the *durations* of beats, rhythm syllables should be based on beat functions rather than on the time values of notes.

And now for the big moment. The unveiling. The moment you've all been waiting for. It gives me great pleasure to introduce...

THE BEAT-FUNCTION SYLLABLE SYSTEM.[16] Here are some examples of how to use it:

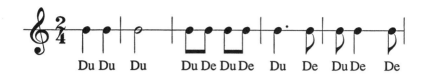

FIGURE 10-9

FIGURE 10-10

---

16 This system of rhythm syllables is sometimes called the "Gordon Syllable System." Gordon, however, did not create it by himself. James Froseth and Albert Blaser also contributed to its construction. I will, therefore, refer to it in this book as the "beat-function syllable system" to avoid any misleading attribution.

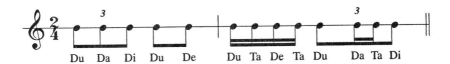

FIGURE 10-11

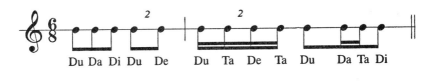

FIGURE 10-12

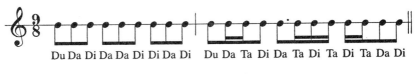

FIGURE 10-13

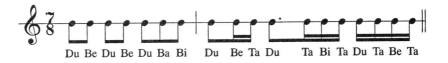

FIGURE 10-14

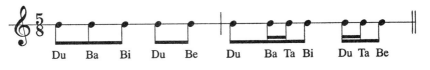

FIGURE 10-15

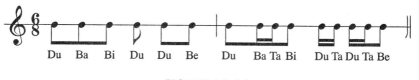

Du Ba Bi Du Du Be   Du Ba Ta Bi   Du Ta Du Ta Be

FIGURE 10-16

Clearly, I've given you an incomplete series of possible patterns; but what could I do? I hope it will give you a good head start with the beat-function syllable system. Try to make up your own patterns for practice. Also, try *not* to read the syllables as a way of learning them. Practice the patterns and the syllables outloud, away from notation; that's the best way to learn them.

While you're practicing these syllables, it might help if you keep certain things in mind. 1) *Du* is pronounced "doo." *De* is pronounced "day." *Da* is pronounced "dah." *Di* is pronounced "dee." *Ta* is pronounced "tah." 2) The macro beats are always *du*, even when they are chanted simultaneously with duple micro beats (*du-de*) or triple micro beats (*du-da-di*). 3) As you can see—and hear—the micro beats are different for duple meter and triple meter. 4) Also, the micro beats are different for unusual meters (*du-be*, for instance, in contrast to *du-de*).

"Where has this been all my life?" will probably be your reaction as you get to know this system better. You'll soon realize that there is virtually no pattern these syllables will not accommodate.

Now, for a change of pace, let's say that the macro beats in duple meter are half notes instead of quarter notes; and let's say that the macro beats in triple meter are dotted half notes instead of dotted quarter notes. And just so there is no confusion (ha!), let me tell you that quarter notes in Figure 10-9 equal the half notes in Figure 10-17. Also the dotted quarter notes in Figure 10-10 equal the dotted half notes in Figure 10-18.

FIGURE 10-17

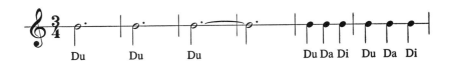

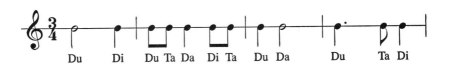

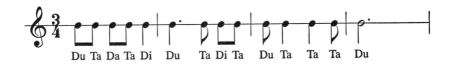

FIGURE 10-18

Well, that's all I have to say about rhythm syllables. Oh, one more thing. This system, as user-friendly as it is, has at least one internal inconsistency that Gordon doesn't talk about. In triple meter, how do you chant divisions *of* divisions? Do you know what I mean? The patterns in Figure 10-19 are easy to deal with; they're simply divisions in triple meter.

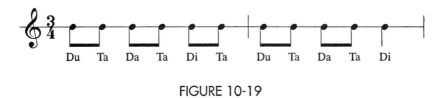

FIGURE 10-19

But what about the patterns in Figure 10-20? Divisions of divisions! This melodic rhythm, incidentally, comes from variation #8 of Bach's *Goldberg Variations*.

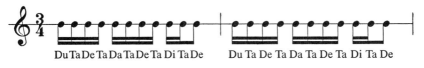

FIGURE 10-20

Fine. But do you see what's happening? In Figure 10-19, divisions are: *Du Ta Da Ta Di Ta*. In Figure 10-20, they are: *Du De Da De Di De*. Which is correct? Answer: Both are correct. It all depends on the circumstances. And *that's* all I have to say about rhythm syllables.

What about the tonal syllable systems? Here they are again: 1) interval-names, 2) numbers, 3) fixed-*do*, 4) movable-*do* with a *do*-based minor, and 5) movable-*do* with a *la*-based minor.

I've already talked about intervals in chapter 5 so there's not much point in talking about them here. I'll just say this: intervals are wonderful things to learn about. . . later; but they make no sense to a student who doesn't have a large vocabulary of *functional* tonal patterns.

The number system is very popular, but it's perhaps the worst tonal system of the five. First of all, it has no chromatic syllables. I suppose you could sing an ascending chromatic scale like this: 1, 1 1/2, 2, 2 1/2, 3. Ah, but what numbers would you use coming *down*? Here's another problem. An ascending diatonic scale is easy to sing using numbers: 1, 2, 3, 4, 5, 6, 7, 1. But how about skipping numbers?

1, 3, 5. Try explaining to even a bright seven-year-old what happened to 2 and 4. And what about skipping numbers backwards? 5, 3, 1. This confuses *me*! Imagine what it would do to a child.

The fixed-do system is also very popular, but it's inconsistent with how we audiate. Consider the two tonic major patterns in Figure 10-21. Both have the same harmonic function, and yet both are assigned different syllables. Since we audiate syntactically—that is, structurally—both patterns should have the same verbal associations. The main problem with the fixed-do system is that, in order to use it, children must learn twelve different verbal associations for patterns that are audiated the same way.

FIGURE 10-21

A friend of mine who tutors music theory students at the Eastman School of Music said to me that he uses fixed-*do* because it helps students to perform atonal music. I suggested to him that the music he calls "atonal" actually has tonal implications. I referred him to a passage from Bernstein's lecture series, *The Unanswered Question* (1976). Here it is:

Schoenberg was the first to renounce the word "atonality," even to deny the *possibility* of atonality. . . . He knew—and we too must learn from him—that if ever a true atonality is to be achieved, some uniquely different basis for it must be found. The rules of the twelve-tone method may be non-universal and even arbitrary, but not arbitrary enough to destroy the inherent tonal relationships among those twelve tones. Perhaps a real atonality can be achieved only artificially, through electronic means, or through a truly arbitrary division of the octave space into something other than the twelve equidistant intervals of our chromatic scale (p. 289).

How does the wild thought strike you that *all* music is ultimately and basically tonal, even when it's "nontonal" (p. 291)?

What interests [me] is the fascinating ambiguity between the planned antitonal functions of the twelve-tone row, and *the inevitable tonal implications that innately reside in it, do what you will* [Italics supplied] (p. 295).

What about the movable *do* system with a *do*-based minor? In order for me to explain properly why this system is inappropriate, I must first define certain words: key, tonality, keyality, key signature, tonal center, tonic, and resting tone. Probably the only word in the list that looks fishy to you is "keyality," a word Gordon coined. All the others, you probably know. Still, let me go over them one at a time.

When people talk about the "key" of a piece of music, they're really talking about three different things: the key signature, the tonality, and the keyality. A key signature, as you know, may include one or more sharps or flats, or none at all. Now, consider the notated key signature of one sharp. Some people, when they think of one sharp, automatically think of G major. But is this necessarily correct? Not at all, when you consider that one sharp could also mean e minor, F# locrian, A dorian, B phrygian, and so on.

Now think of the term "G major." It has two parts: the "G" part and the "major" part. The "major" part is easy to account for. That's the tonality. Major is a tonality; minor is a tonality; dorian, phrygian, lydian. These are all tonalities. And what is the "G" part? That, Gordon calls the keyality. If you were to spontaneously sing "Happy Birthday," you would naturally make every effort to sing it in major tonality. Your choice of keyality—Eb, F, G, Ab, and so on—would be more or less arbitrary. Even though tonality is basic to your audiation, you must audiate both tonality and keyality to perform "Happy Birthday" correctly. To sum up: you audiate tonalities and keyalities; you see key signatures.

But that's not all. The term "tonal center" has two meanings. Imagine two pieces of music, one in D major, the other in E flat major. Because both pieces are in major tonality, they both have the same *relative* tonal center: the first degree of the major scale. Right? Now here's where things get tricky. A piece in D major has the specific tonal center of D; a piece in E flat major has the specific tonal center of E flat. In light of that, is it correct to say that both pieces have the same tonal center? Yes and no.

To avoid this confusion, Gordon uses two different words in place of the expression "tonal center." The words are "resting tone" and "tonic."

The fundamental pitch of a tonality—the first degree of the scale—is the resting tone.

The pitches E flat and D are tonics.

So a piece in D major and a piece in E flat major both have the same resting tone, even though the tonics are different; and a piece in D major and a piece in d minor both have the same tonic, even though the resting tones are different. Get it? To sum up: resting tones go with tonalities; tonics go with keyalities.

Now then. What about so-called "atonal" music? Gordon (1993) has suggested that the music of the Second Viennese School is not "atonal", but rather "multitonal" and "multikeyal." There is not an absence of a resting tone or a tonic; rather there are, as a given piece develops, *many* resting tones and tonics that are rapidly changing. The catch is that no two listeners may agree about what tonality or keyality the piece is in at any given moment. The various tonalities and keyalities are often subjective.[17]

---

17 I once mentioned to Gordon that, since he was so fond of coining new terms, he should make room for two more in the next edition of his book: **tonalic rhythm** and **keyalic rhythm.** I suggested that there are moments in multitonal music during which the

What does all this have to do with the choice of a tonal solfège system? A great deal. Try an experiment. Improvise in D major for about ten minutes. Just sing tunes to yourself. Really get centered in D major. Then sing the dominant pattern in Figure 10-22A and resolve it by singing a D. Enjoy it. Let that dominant pattern and resolution really resonate. Next, wait about five minutes. Then start to improvise melodies in d minor, again, for a solid ten minutes. Flood your ears with d minor. Then sing the dominant pattern in Figure 10-22B and resolve it by singing a D.

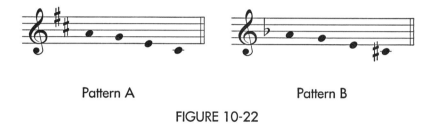

Pattern A   Pattern B

FIGURE 10-22

Weird, huh? Do you sense that both dominants are somehow different from each other? I know I do. Even though they *sound* the same, they're still *different*. But how? Phonologically they're the same, but syntactically they're different; or perhaps it's fair to say that *quantitatively* they're the same, but *qualitatively* they're different.

However you say it, you cannot ignore it. A dominant pattern in major tonality is different from a dominant pattern in minor tonality, and that's that. Actually, that's not only that: a tonic resolution of the note D in major is qualitatively different from a tonic resolution of D in minor. Same pitch; different . . .ambiance.

For these reasons, *do*-based minor is out. Quite frankly, it plays

tonal centers change *more rapidly than at other times.* Just as harmonic rhythm refers to the rate of change of harmony, tonalic rhythm could refer to the rate of change of tonality; and keyalic rhythm could refer to the rate of change of key tricks with our audiation. Perhaps you believe that the do-based minor system can be used to teach the characteristic tones in a tonality, such as the flatted third and the flatted sixth in minor. The problem is that we don't audiate those characteristic tones as isolated phonological events; we audiate them as they relate to a resting tone. *Do*-based minor—in fact, *do*-based dorian, mixolydian, etc.—will lead students to believe that songs in tonalities other than major *are still in major but with chromatic alterations.*

As I said before, the only tonal system that is consistent with how we audiate is movable-*do* with a *la*-based minor.[18] I can imagine you shaking your head. All I can say is: Try it. With a little practice you'll learn to like it. "But suppose I don't?" you may be thinking. "Do I *really* have to use movable-*do* with a *la*-based minor? And do I *really* have to use a beat-function rhythm syllable system?"

Only if you want to teach audiation.

After your students have learned to associate syllables with patterns, they can begin to use their knowledge of tonal and rhythm solfège in traditional classroom activities.

Suppose your students have learned to sing the resting tone in minor tonality (*la*) as part of their pattern instruction. They can now be taught to audiate and sing the resting tone of a familiar rote song in minor tonality with solfège.

Another example: suppose that your students have learned, during pattern instruction, to perform macro and micro beats in triple meter with beat-function syllables. They can now learn to "find" and name those beat functions in familiar songs and chants in triple meter.

18The moveable *do* system has at least one internal inconsistency: *Re* and *ra* should be switched. The descending chromatic syllables are *te, le, se, me,* **ra**. Clearly, *ra* doesn't belong. Also, the diatonic syllable *re* should be *ra* in keeping with other diatonic syllables *fa* and *la*.

Step Three: Partial Synthesis

Partial synthesis is a ridiculous name for this level of learning: there's nothing "partial" about it. Gordon calls it a "synthesis" because, at this point, children learn the syntactic meaning of a *series* of familiar patterns without notation. He contrasts partial synthesis with composite synthesis, a more advanced level of learning, in which children learn the syntactic meaning of a series of *notated* patterns. I still don't believe that this distinction justifies the use of the confusing word "partial." Better to call it *pattern* synthesis. That is, after all, what's going on.

At this level, the teacher sings or chants the same patterns she taught at the aural/oral and verbal association levels. This time, children hear the patterns not in isolation but in a series, and children learn the tonality or meter of that series. Also children compare the tonalities and meters of at least two different series of patterns, a more difficult task than simply naming the tonality or meter of a single series.

Three other characteristics of partial synthesis are worth noting. First, the teacher does not need to establish tonality or meter. The series of patterns itself provides the syntactic context. Second, the teacher *should not use tonal or rhythm solfège*. Theoretically, those tools have served their purpose. Third, the teacher still teaches by rote at this level. Children should not be made to infer tonality or meter.

How does this level of learning fit into the whole-part-whole learning process? That's difficult to say. At the aural/oral and verbal association levels, children are clearly delving into the "parts" of music. At this level, they're learning that the whole is greater, or at least different, from the sum of its parts.

Two new musical elements come into play at this level of learning: modulation and form. And, of course, there are many ways to teach these elements.

Teachers could explain the type of tonal modulation occurring in a familiar rote song. They could then ask students to sing the changing resting tones or tonics with the appropriate syllables. Or, if the modulation is metrical, teachers could tell students what kind of metrical change is occurring; students could then be taught to find the appropriate macro and micro beats as the song modulates.

Teachers could also explain the form of the rote song and have students confirm it by singing or chanting repeated or contrasting patterns in the song.

Step Four: Symbolic Association

At this point, children learn to read and write tonal and rhythm notation with the aid of solfège. Interestingly, the way children learn to read is the opposite of the way they learn to write. Here's what happens when they read: first they see notation; then they associate the notation with solfège; then they associate solfège with sounds; and then they read. When they write, the process works in reverse: first they audiate the music they want to write; then they associate that music with solfège; then they associate solfège with notation; and then they write.

Think of the two processes as chain reactions with solfège as the vital link in the chains.

These ideas about music notation are Gordon's, and I agree with him up to this point; but I believe, quite frankly, that his ideas about reading and writing are the weakest parts of his work.

Briefly, I believe that many of Gordon's ideas about teaching music notation are theoretically unsound because he underrates the importance of musical phonology; sometimes he even confuses it with music theory. This confusion has led him to leave out a crucial step in his skill learning sequence: **Children should, at some point, learn to read isolated pitches and durations—that is, *parts* of patterns.** I am certainly *not* referring to the names of the lines and spaces on the staff, or to the letter names of notes, or to the names of time values. I agree with Gordon that children need not learn these theoretical facts in order to learn to read and write music notation.

Rather, I'm suggesting that children learn the musical equivalent of phonics. As you'll see when you read about the generalization-symbolic level, children will not be able to read unfamiliar patterns without this skill. Specifically, they will lack the essential ability to decode notation.[19]

Of course, I'm just speculating. I have no proof that I'm right. But let's assume that I am. What new problems will this added level of learning create? One problem immediately comes to mind: because of the phonological differences between the tonal and rhythm dimensions of music, tonal and rhythm notation cannot be taught the same way. Let me explain:

A tonal pattern can be broken up into its phonological elements—isolated pitches—and then those pitches can be synthesized back into their original pattern without any change in sound occurring. A G sharp always sounds like a G sharp in spite of the many syntactic changes it may go through.

With rhythm, this is not so. Students will not know the sound of an isolated duration unless it is placed in a specific rhythmic context. Or to put it another way: How long is a quarter note? Answer: Compared to what? Precisely! That's the point. Durations are relative. So how does one teach rhythm notation phonologically?

Here's what I suggest: Perhaps the equivalent of "synthetic" phonics can be used for tonal reading. On the other hand, an "analytic" phonics approach seems more appropriate for rhythm reading.

The procedure for teaching tonal notation might be this: First establish tonality and keyality. Then write a treble clef with the appropriate key signature. Then teach students the lines or spaces where they can find *do*, *mi*, and *so*. (Don't forget to sing the syllables rather

---

[19] Many linguists such as Flesch (1955), Smith (1985 and 1988), and Samuels (1971) agree that knowledge of the alphabet is *not* crucial for learning to read English. In fact, it may actually be a hindrance in early phonics instruction (Flesch 1955, p. 28). Knowledge of letter names and of the alphabet are examples of theoretical understanding; and they should not be confused with phonics, which is symbolic association.

than speak them. Also you won't need to write the syllables. Just sing and point.) Then point to one line or space and ask your students, one at a time, to sing the pitch that the line or space represents with the appropriate solfège syllable. Once your students can do this successfully, you might write whole tonic major patterns on the blackboard, sing them, then point to *one note* in a pattern, and ask one student at a time to read and sing that note with the appropriate syllable. Once students can read parts of tonal patterns, they are ready to read whole tonal patterns.

Rhythm reading is a bit more complicated. The procedure for teaching rhythm notation might be this: Establish tempo and meter. Write the appropriate measure signature on the blackboard. Write a rhythm pattern with the equivalent of two underlying macro beats. Put the complex melodic rhythm on the first macro beat. Then perform the pattern for students while everyone patches duple or triple micro beats (depending, of course, on the meter). Call on one student at a time to chant the pattern with rhythm syllables. Then reverse the macro beats. In other words, write a pattern with the complex melodic rhythm on the *second* macro beat, and ask one student at a time to chant it with rhythm syllables while everyone patches micro beats. Then combine the complex parts of two patterns into one pattern. For instance, instead of asking students to read pattern A or B in Figure 10-23, ask them to read pattern C.

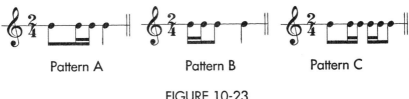

Pattern A   Pattern B   Pattern C

FIGURE 10-23

Before I move on to the next level of learning, let me say a few brief words about phonics instruction in language reading. From 1912 to 1981, 124 studies compared the results of systematic phonics instruction with either "incidental" phonics or no phonics instruction. Most of the comparative studies followed a basic design: after two groups of children had received sufficient (though different) reading instruction, they were tested for word recognition skill. After the mid-1950s, children were tested, almost invariably, for both word recognition and paragraph comprehension skills (Walcutt and McCracken, 1974 [Chapters on research and evaluation by Robert Dykstra.]).

The results of these studies, with very few exceptions, explicitly favored comprehensive, systematic phonics instruction (Gurren and Hughes 1965, Chall 1967, Dykstra 1974, Flesch 1955 and 1981). For instance, Chall (1967, p. 307), after surveying 85 studies, concluded:

> The research from 1912 to 1965 indicates that a code-emphasis [phonics-first] method—i.e. one that views beginning reading as essentially different from mature reading and emphasizes learning of the printed code for the spoken language—produces better results, at least up to the point where sufficient evidence seems to be available, the end of third grade.
>
> The results are better, not only in terms of the mechanical aspects of literacy alone, as was once supposed, but also in terms of the ultimate goal of reading instruction—comprehension and possibly even speed of reading. The long existing fear that an initial code-emphasis produces readers who do not read for meaning or with enjoyment is unfounded.

The phonics approach that Chall is referring to is called synthetic phonics. It works like this: Children learn isolated phonic items—the sounds that go with symbols—and then they learn how these phonic items are combined to form words. According to Chall (1983), synthetic phonics has achieved far greater success than analytic phonics, in which children begin with whole words, then analyze them, then re-combine the phonological elements to form other words.

This may strike you as odd. Analytic phonics, you may be thinking, should have achieved greater success than it has. After all, it *seems* to be a whole-part-whole approach. Actually it isn't. Imagine the first "whole" to be a child's aural language development and the building of a large language vocabulary. The next "part" is symbolic association—that is, the association of isolated sounds with isolated symbols. The final "whole" is the ability to decode words and understand them, to take phonological information *from* the page in order to bring understanding *to* the page. In light of this, synthetic phonics is a whole-part-whole approach; whereas analytic phonics is a whole-*whole*-part-whole approach. Clearly there is one "whole" too many.

I find it ironic that analytic phonics, which has *not* had great success as an approach to teaching language reading, may turn out to be the key to teaching rhythm notation.

Perhaps some readers of this book—those who are committed to Music Learning Theory in its present form—are disturbed by what I have written. I think it's worth pointing out that Music Learning Theory, with all its present complexities, is just now in its infancy, and will grow to maturity only after many more years of research.

Step Five: Composite Synthesis

At the composite synthesis level, children learn to read and write different series of familiar patterns and are taught the syntactic meaning of those series.

I'll be frank: I believe this level of learning is unnecessary.

Certainly there is a difference between reading patterns and reading a series of patterns with comprehension, just as, in language, there is a difference between reading words and reading a paragraph with comprehension. But Gordon's skill learning sequence is designed so that this skill should simply come naturally to students.

After all, they have already learned to audiate syntax at the partial synthesis level; and they have already learned to read at the symbolic association level. What more do they need? Must they relearn syntax? Must they relearn how to read? My belief is that, just as Gordon underrates the importance of phonology, he overrates the importance of this level of learning.

Certainly it's a possible exercise: You write a series of patterns on the blackboard—the same patterns you've been teaching all along—perhaps in an unfamiliar order. You read and sing or chant the series with a neutral syllable. You ask children to read it and sing or chant it with a neutral syllable. And you review that the series is in major or minor tonality, or duple or triple meter.

Step Six: Generalization

Generalization is a level of inference learning, and this fact alone implies two things. First, children are not taught anything by rote at this level; they make their own discoveries. Second, their success at making inferences depends largely on the quality of rote learning they have received.

If you're teaching students at the generalization-aural/oral level, you might sing two patterns for them and ask the children whether the patterns were same or different.

If you're teaching students at the generalization-verbal level, you might sing (with a neutral syllable such as "bah") two unfamiliar tonal patterns—a dominant pattern and a tonic pattern in major tonality perhaps—and ask the children to tell you in what specific way they are different. After that, you might ask the children to sing those patterns with solfège syllables. You might also sing or chant a series of unfamiliar patterns with a neutral syllable and ask students to identify the tonality or meter of that series. Finally, you might sing or chant two different series of unfamiliar patterns—one in major tonality and one in minor tonality perhaps—and ask students to explain how the patterns modulate.

At the generalization-symbolic level, children read unfamiliar patterns (sight-read, in other words) and write unfamiliar patterns from dictation. Some supporters of Music Learning Theory believe that children must first learn how to read a series of *familiar* patterns in order to sight-read *unfamiliar* patterns accurately with comprehension. I don't agree. I suspect that there are better ways to prepare students for sight reading. Here are three suggestions:

1. Make sure that you teach symbolic association—that is, decoding—thoroughly.

2. Make sure that your students are reasonably successful at the generalization-verbal level.

   The nature of generalization learning is that the emphasis is not on you, the teacher, imparting information; rather, it is on the students teaching themselves. Therefore you will have much less control over your students' success at this level than you have had in the past. Still, if most of your students can accomplish tasks at the generalization-verbal level—if they can understand the syntactic meaning of a series of unfamiliar patterns with the use of solfège—then they are ready to learn to sight-read.

3. Make sure—and this one is crucial—that the "unfamiliar" patterns that you ask your students to read are not completely outside their experience.

   Let me elaborate on this last point. Unfamiliarity is absolute. When something's unfamiliar to you, it's unfamiliar and that's that. But when something is familiar, who can say just *how* familiar it is? Familiarity is a matter of degree. If your students have learned six tonic patterns in minor tonality, and are then asked to make inferences about a seventh tonic minor pattern, is it correct to say that the new tonic minor pattern is unfamiliar? Not at all. It's merely *less* familiar to students than the patterns you taught by rote.

What I'm suggesting is this: if your students have learned tonic, dominant, and subdominant patterns by rote, then don't ask them to make inferences about chromatic or modulatory patterns. Play fair: use "unfamiliar" patterns with familiar functions. I'm sure that your students will find this challenging enough.

Several pages back I said that your students would not be able to read unfamiliar patterns at the generalization-symbolic level unless they were taught to decode notation. Let's say that your students have learned to read pattern A in Figure 10-24 by rote. Without decoding skill—the ability to associate isolated sounds with isolated symbols with the aid of solfège—how could your students sight-read pattern B successfully, a pattern they have never seen before? My question is not: How could they understand pattern B syntactically? If they've achieved success at the generalization-verbal level, then I'm sure they'd understand the pattern in context *if someone else read it for them*. My question is: Without the ability to decode, what skills would enable them to read the pattern for themselves?

Many of Gordon's ideas about teaching music notation come from a field of language study called psycholinguistics. Since I disagree with many of Gordon's ideas about teaching notation—and since many of them come from this field—I think it would be worthwhile for me now to explain some of the underlying principles of psycholinguistics in detail.

Pattern A   Pattern B

FIGURE 10-24

115

My first encounter with any psycholinguistic idea occurred about eleven years ago when I was an undergraduate. At the time, my major was not music education but cultural anthropology! I came across a fascinating passage in the book *The Silent Billion Speak* by Frank Laubach (1945). In this book, Laubach describes his work in the Philippines and his attempt to learn the Maranaw language. He writes (p. 23):

> When we tried to write the words we heard, nobody could tell us where one word began and another ended! If I asked Pambaya, "What is the Maranaw word for 'go?'" he did not know. But if I asked how to say, "Where are you going?" he answered at once, "Andakasoong." By many trials and errors, we discovered that *anda* was "where," *ka* was "you" and *soong* was "go"—"Where you go?"

This passage suggested something startling to me: we do not form sentences by synthesizing words; we discover words by analyzing sentences. Could it be, then, that we think with sentences rather than with words? Are words nothing but artificial constructs for notational convenience? Some evidence supports this notion (Ehri, Barron and Feldman, 1978). Children who have not yet learned to read have difficulty segmenting sentences into words; when they see words separated by white space on a page, they quickly begin to understand their nature.

Now for the big question: If the ultimate goal of reading is to comprehend an author's thoughts, and if thoughts are not conveyed necessarily through words (or even through a series of words), then why do teachers insist that students develop word recognition skills, possibly at the expense of meaning identification skills? The issues raised in this question are the basis for psycholinguistic thinking.

According to Frank Smith (1979), one of the most prominent psycholinguists and one of Gordon's most influential sources, there are two primary theories of reading: outside-in theories and inside-out theories. Outside-in theories "view reading as a process that begins with the print and ends with some representation or interpretation inside the brain" (p. 31). Clearly, the systematic phonics and whole-word approaches are based on an outside-in theory. In contrast, an inside-out theory, or psycholinguistic perspective "perceives reading as a highly discriminative process that begins in the brain and ends with selective attention to only part of the printed text" (p. 31).

According to Smith (1988), the more information we can bring to the page, the less information we need to take from the page. This paradox is crucial, Smith asserts (1985), because the brain cannot possibly process all the information supplied by the printed page; instead, the mind processes the *essentialness* of what is on the page or, in Smith's terms, the "distinctive features" of print.

To further this argument, Smith (1988) makes a distinction between *surface structure* and *deep structure*. Surface structure is the visual information of written language and the phonological information of spoken language; deep structure is the meaning of language. Smith (1988, p.26) states that "meaning lies beyond the mere sounds or printed marks of language, and cannot be derived from surface structure by any simple or mechanistic process."

One of the most fascinating aspects of Smith's work is his theory of how readers make predictions when they read. His main point is that skilled readers predict the meaning of the text they are about to read without necessarily predicting specific words. He states (1985, p. 28):

> If you could predict every word exactly, there would be no purpose in reading the passage in the first place. But what is necessary is that every time you are always able to make a *reasonable* guess about the next word. You do not predict recklessly. You select from a relatively small set of *possible* words in the particular context, and as a result cut down the number of alternatives among which the brain has to select.

Perhaps the most disturbing of Smith's theories is that a reading learning hierarchy cannot be constructed; skills cannot be analyzed and sequenced. "Children," Smith writes (1988, p. 205), "do not learn to read from programs. In particular, they cannot learn from the more structured, systematic 'reading skills' programs where every supposed learning step is predetermined for the child."

For the student of Music Learning Theory, this is a shocking bit of information! Smith's theories are in direct contrast to Gagné's opinions about reading instruction. This next quote comes from a correspondence between Flesch and Gagné that was printed in Flesch's book *Why Johnny Still Can't Read* (1981, pp. 35-36). Gagné writes:

> The objective at the decoding stage of learning is to enable the child to say orally such a word as *concatenation*, which he has never seen or heard before. *Whether he knows the meaning of the word is quite irrelevant.* [Italics supplied] The all-important capability he is acquiring at this stage is the ability to say, when he sees it in print, the word *concatenation* in a way that is discriminably different to him from the printed word *concentration*.
>
> In an adult, the difficulties experienced with a novel word provide a fairly sure clue to the existence of a gap in his early instruction. . . .On the first encounter, he may be unable to read a word like *obsequiousness*, which, to an individual who has learned to identify sounds, is ridiculously simple.

Robert Gagné and Frank Smith are clearly two of Gordon's most influential sources. But how does Gordon reconcile the fact that Gagné—an ardent phonics advocate—and Smith disagree, not only about reading instruction but about learning in general?

My belief is that future music learning theorists will find Smith's work extremely valuable, particularly as they grapple with the nature of inference learning, predictions in notational audiation, and the relationship between surface structure and deep structure. In short, Smith makes splendid sense to me—provided his subject is *not* symbolic association or learning theory.

Step Seven: Creativity and Improvisation

In the first chapter of his provocative book *The Art of Clear Thinking* (1951), the linguist Rudolf Flesch tries to answer the question, What is thinking? The chapter is called "Robots, Apes, and You." He develops this chapter by discussing 1) the infallible memory of computers and 2) the insights of chimpanzees and the origins of Gestalt psychology. He concludes the chapter by stating:

> . . .the gap is narrowing: the animals' insight can be traced back to memory and [computers] may eventually be trained to solve problems by insight.
>
> Midway between the ape brain and the machine brain is the one you carry in your head. It's a reasonable guess that it works similarly to the other two—those two brains science has shown to be so much alike. If so, it's proper to call your brain a memory machine; what you do—whether you play a game of canasta or write The Great American Novel—is to solve problems by the application of past experience.
>
> So here is your definition of thinking: It is the manipulation of memories (p. 8).

What has this to do with musical creativity? A great deal. One must have a stock of tonal and rhythm patterns (musical memories) to manipulate in order to create music.

Perhaps you disagree. Maybe you've seen or read about young children "creating" patterns on a barred instrument in pentatonic. But were those children *audiating* what they were performing? In other words, were they "inner hearing with comprehension" the music they were about to perform before they actually played? Probably not. So, were they creating after all? If not, what were they doing? Probably they were just exploring; and, strictly speaking, exploration is not creativity. In fact, Gordon (1993) makes a distinction between *three* words that are usually used interchangeably: exploration, creativity, and improvisation.

Exploration is just that. If a child plays on a xylophone and has no idea what she's doing, she is not creating; she's exploring. But it makes sense that she must explore before she can create.

Creativity, Flesch might say, is the manipulation of (musical) memories.

Improvisation is creativity with restrictions. I might say to my students, "I'll sing a *tonic* major pattern, but I'd like you to sing back a *dominant* major pattern." Notice that I'm not telling them which dominant major pattern they must sing; they're still free to choose, but within specific parameters.

Perhaps you think that this distinction between creativity and improvisation is nothing but pedantic hair-splitting. Well, in a way it is. *All* creative artists impose restrictions on themselves. How could they create if they didn't? So then: where does creativity end and improvisation begin? I suspect there's no single answer that will satisfy everyone. The best I can do is suggest to you what Gordon has suggested to me: the two exist on a continuum. As you "invent" new musical structures, the more restrictions you are faced with, the more you're improvising; the fewer restriction you're faced with, the more you're creating—up to a point, of course. After all, you cannot create without at least a few restrictions. For instance, you can't simply "let the music flow out of you" without first choosing a meter, tempo, tonality, and keyality to create in.

Actually, I find the distinction between creativity and improvisation only mildly interesting. What *really* interests me is the fact that neither creativity nor improvisation just happens. Without a foundation of patterns learned by rote, no artist could create.

Do you remember, way back in chapter 2, I discussed the whole-part-whole learning process? I said that rote learning is the emphasis of the first "whole" and the next "part." I described the final "whole" as a payoff. What did I mean by that? For me, creativity is the payoff; it's the best way, the most direct and satisfying way, to understand and appreciate music. Listening to and performing Bach's music can help you understand 18th-century harmony and counterpoint to a certain extent; but imagine how much greater your understanding would be if you tried writing a fugue yourself!

And now we come to a thorny problem: Many music teachers I know are downright scared of this level of learning. "What?!" they scream. "Are you suggesting that *I* create music? Who do you think I am, Beethoven?"

In his book *How To Write* (1943, pp. 26-27), the humorist Stephen Leacock describes a similar fear among writers:

> Suppose a would-be writer can't begin. I really believe there are many excellent writers who have never written because they never could begin. This is especially the case of people of great sensitiveness, or of people of advanced education. Professors suffer most of all from this inhibition. Many of them carry their unwritten books to the grave. *They overestimate the magnitude of the task; they overestimate the greatness of the final result* [Italics supplied]. A child in a "prep" school will write "The History of Greece" and fetch it home finished after school. "He wrote a fine history of Greece the other day," says his proud father. Thirty years later the child, grown to be a professor, dreams of writing the History of Greece—the whole of it from the first Ionic invasion of the Aegean to the downfall of Alexandria. But he dreams. He never starts. He can't. It's too big.
>
> The best practical advice that can be given on this subject is, don't *start*. That is, don't start anywhere in particular. Begin at the end; begin in the middle, but *begin*. If you like, you can fool yourself by pretending that the start you make isn't really the beginning, and that you are going to write it all over again. Pretend that what you write is just a note, a fragment, a nothing. Only get started.

Great advice, isn't it? Don't feel that you must compose a four-movement symphony! Instead, choose any tonality or meter you want, and then create a song. . .four bars long. . .eight bars long. Just string a few patterns together. Before you know it, you'll have a song on your hands. And don't think that the finished product must be brilliant. Don't "overestimate the magnitude of the task, the greatness of the final result." Relax. Create.

Are you disappointed by what I've written? Perhaps you believe that musical creativity is a glamorous, mystical form of artistic expression. Certainly, you say, there must be more to it than simply "stringing patterns together." Sure there is: excitement, agony, catharsis, frustration, ecstasy—and ultimately comradery. For what better way is there for you to move closer to Beethoven, to Handel, to Bach, and to their music, than to understand what it *feels* like to compose?

But yes, to get back to the point, I *am* trying to demystify musical creativity. Where there's mysticism, there's fear, and who needs that? On the other hand, I would *never* say, as Gordon has said, that creativity may not exist at all. *Of course* it exists.

Let Harold Kushner (1981, pp. 51-52) make my point for me:

> This is what it means to create: not to make something out of nothing, but to make order out of chaos. A creative scientist or historian does not make up facts but orders facts; he sees connections between them rather than seeing them as random data. A creative writer does not make up new words but arranges familiar words in patterns which say something fresh to us.

It follows then, that a creative musician doesn't make up new pitches or durations; rather, she faces this challenge: to make up new arrangements of the same pitches and durations available to everyone else.

What an exciting level of learning this is! Imagine your students creating melodies, improvising realizations of a figured bass, and, someday perhaps, composing fugues and symphonies. I appeal to the teachers and administrators reading this book: LET'S MAKE THIS HAPPEN!

Step Eight: Theoretical Understanding

Music theory is like grammar in language. You don't speak grammar; you speak English. But you can talk about English by explaining its grammar.

The question is: Why bother to learn grammar if you can already speak and make yourself understood? In his book *How To Make Sense* (1954), Rudolf Flesch has written a fascinating chapter called "Is Grammar Necessary?" He writes (pp. 22-24):

A large part of your life was spent in learning English grammar and usage.

What did you get out of it? How often do you use your precious knowledge of moods and tenses, participles and gerunds, demonstrative pronouns, and subordinating conjunctions?

The obvious answer is, Never. You speak, read, write all day long, but throughout your adult life you haven't spent a single second in deciding whether to put a verb in the indicative or the subjunctive, or in exercising a choice between a definite and an indefinite article. Grammar is something you learn, promptly forget, and dismiss for the rest of your life.

Why should this be so? How did it come about that a considerable part of your school learning was devoted to something so utterly useless? Once you start to think about it, you immediately realize that here is one of the biggest mysteries of our civilization. . . .

The vast majority of mankind would consider this procedure completely crazy and incomprehensible. You learn how to use words; then you use them. What else is there to study? Ask an African or a South Sea Islander—anyone unspoiled by Western habits of thought—and he will look at you in astonishment. He has learned how to master his native tongue; as far as he is concerned, grammar doesn't come into it. Correctness, purity of speech—what does it all mean?

Of course with us this whole idea is so ingrained that we are embarrassed and disconcerted when someone raises such a question in polite society. Children must learn grammar because otherwise they would grow up without having learned grammar. . . .It's completely illogical; the whole thing falls to pieces after five minutes of consecutive thought. And yet we all hang onto it for dear life as one of the mainstays of our educational system.

What makes this passage so extraordinary—apart from Flesch's brilliant mind and scintillating prose style—is that it applies to music as well as to language. Substitute the words "music theory" in place of the word "grammar" and you have a description of our situation. One of the biggest mistakes we make is that we overrate the importance of music theory. Recall what I said in chapter 4: Music theory is music that doesn't exist either acoustically or audiationally; it's all talk—talk about voice leading, talk about intervals, talk about scales, talk about the circle of fifths, talk about chord structure. I must admit, I love music theory, mainly because I love to talk.

Let's first teach our students to audiate, to perform, to read, to write, to create, and to improvise. In other words, let's give *them* something to talk about.

Building A Curriculum

There you have it. Eight levels of learning. Everything you always wanted to know about Music Learning Theory—almost.

You still don't know how to combine skills and content; and you still don't know how to "bridge," that is, how to make temporary skips, from one level to another. Both are very easy. Just follow these three rules: 1) Introduce every new bit of content (major tonality, duple meter, etc.), without exception, at the aural/oral level; 2) Don't skip any level of discrimination (rote) learning; 3) Bridge to a level of inference learning, if you choose to, only after students have been exposed to its counterpart in discrimination learning.

Let's say that you wanted to teach chromatic patterns in minor tonality. At what skill level do you start? At the aural/oral level of course. Imagine what would happen if you started at the verbal association level. Your students would have to learn to audiate patterns, perform patterns, and apply solfège to patterns all at the same time. Clearly this would be beyond the capability of most of your students. So always start at the aural/oral level. And certainly don't skip from the aural/oral level to a higher level of discrimination learning.

Imagine this: You could be teaching chromatic patterns at the aural/oral level and tonic and dominant at the symbolic association level. Are you beginning to see the possibilities that Music Learning Theory offers you?

Let's say that you've taught tonic and dominant patterns in major and minor tonalities at the aural/oral level. Must you teach those patterns at the verbal association level? Eventually yes. But you may decide to ask your students to generalize or to create with that content first. The catch is: you may bridge only to the generalization-aural/oral level, or to the creativity-aural/oral level; you may *not* bridge to the generalization-verbal level, or to the creativity-aural/oral level with verbal association. Why not? Because you haven't taught that content at the verbal association level yet. Get it? If not, don't

125

feel discouraged. Read through the exercises in Chapter 11 and try to make sense out of them.

In the mean time, imagine this: During the *same month*, your students may be improvising tonic and dominant patterns, learning to sing subdominant patterns with solfège syllables, and learning cadential patterns with a neutral syllable.

Now do you believe that there are tens-of-thousands of methods that can grow out of learning theory?

I started this chapter by listing eight theoretical levels of learning. I'll finish it by listing ten practical guidelines for designing a learning method.

1. Don't begin pattern instruction until your students are ready for it.

2. Once children are ready for pattern instruction, divide each class period between pattern instruction and traditional classroom activities (rote songs, circle games, Orff instruments, and so on).

3. During pattern instruction, keep tonal and rhythm content separate.

4. During pattern instruction, teach one new bit of content at a time, one skill at a time.

5. During pattern instruction, introduce every new bit of content, without exception, at the aural/oral level.

6. Don't skip any level of discrimination (rote) learning.

7. Over several months of instruction, alternate frequently from one tonality to another, from one meter to another.

8. Don't make your comprehensive objectives too burden-some. Aim for about ten sequential objectives per comprehensive objective. Better to have too few than too many.

9. Bridge to a level of inference learning, if you choose to, only after students have been exposed to its counterpart in discrimination learning.

10. When you bridge to a level of inference learning, don't use content that is completely outside the students' experience.

Part Three

Curriculum In Action

CHAPTER 11
Tonal and Rhythm Objectives

I hear the sound I love,
the sound of the human voice,
I hear all sounds running together,
combined, fused or following. . .

—Walt Whitman,
Song of Myself

Plan your work; then work your plan.

—My Father

These exercises make up a reading readiness program.

The challenge for me has been to reconcile two seemingly contradictory ideas: 1) children should not learn to read and write music notation until they're ready; and 2) children should learn to read and write music notation as soon as possible.

I've written 69 rhythm exercises and 64 tonal exercises with these two points in mind. After children complete these exercises they are ready to begin to learn to read and write.

Music education is not a "race against time." We should teach thoroughly, not quickly. On the other hand, music literacy is so much a part of musical independence that to delay the teaching of notation would be unfair to our students.

Let me emphasize that these exercises are not written in stone.

I'm sure I'll reconsider many of my objectives before the '94/'95 school year is over. Or perhaps you'll think of better ones yourself.

Tonal Units and Comprehensive Objectives

Unit 1—Aural/Oral (Exercises 1-6)
Objective: Students will sing, with a neutral syllable, tonic and dominant patterns in major and minor tonalities.

Unit 2—Verbal Association (Exercises 7-13)
Objective: Students will name and sing with solfège syllables the same major patterns they were taught in Unit 1.

Unit 3—Generalization-Verbal (Exercises 14-16)
Objective: Students will sing, with solfège syllables, tonic and dominant patterns in major tonality. The teacher will sing with a neutral syllable.

Unit 4—Verbal Association (Exercises 17-23)
Objective: Students will name and sing with solfège syllables the same minor patterns they were taught in Unit 1.

Unit 5—Generalization-Verbal (Exercises 24-26)
Objective: Students will sing, with solfège syllables, tonic and dominant patterns in minor tonality. The teacher will sing with a neutral syllable.

Unit 6—Aural/Oral (Exercises 27-30)
Objective: Students will sing, with a neutral syllable, subdominant patterns in major and minor tonalities.

Unit 7—Verbal Association (Exercises 31-36)
Objective: Students will name and sing with solfège syllables the same patterns they were taught in Unit 6.

Unit 8—Creativity (Exercises 37-40)
Objective: Students will create patterns with a neutral syllable in

133

response to tonic, dominant, and subdominant patterns in major and minor tonalities sung by the teacher.

Unit 9—Partial Synthesis (Exercises 41-43)

Objective: Students will recognize different *series* of tonic, dominant, and subdominant patterns as being in major or minor tonality.

Unit 10—Generalization-Verbal (Exercises 44-50)

Objective: Students will sing, with solfège syllables, tonic, dominant, and subdominant patterns in major and minor tonalities. The teacher will sing with a neutral syllable.

Unit 11—Improvisation (Exercises 51-64)

Objective: Students will improvise, with solfège syllables, tonic, dominant, and subdominant patterns in major and minor tonalities.

Unit 1: Aural/Oral
(All singing is done with a neutral syllable.)

Sequential Objectives:

1. The student sings the resting tone of patterns in major tonality. (The patterns the teacher sings must be dominant major, then tonic major ending on the resting tone.)
2. The student sings the resting tone of patterns in minor tonality. (The patterns the teacher sings must be dominant minor, then tonic minor ending on the resting tone.)
3. The student sings tonic major patterns.
4. The student sings dominant major patterns.
5. The student sings tonic minor patterns.
6. The student sings dominant minor patterns.

Unit 2: Verbal Association
(All singing is done with solfège syllables)

Sequential Objectives:

    7. The student sings the resting tone in major tonality *(do)*. (The patterns the teacher sings must be dominant major, then tonic major ending on the resting tone.)

    8. The student recognizes patterns with the syllables *do, mi,* and *so* as tonic major patterns.

    9. The student recognizes patterns with the syllables *ti, re, fa,* and *so* as dominant major patterns.

    10. The student discriminates between tonic major patterns and dominant major patterns.

    11. The students name the harmonic functions of the following tonic major and dominant major patterns:

        1. Tonic major/Dominant major;

        2. Dominant major/Tonic major.

    12. The student sings tonic major patterns.

    13. The student sings dominant major patterns.

Unit 3: Generalization-Verbal
(The teacher sings with a neutral syllable; the students sing with solfège syllables.)

Sequential Objectives:

    14. The student identifies the harmonic functions of one familiar and one unfamiliar pattern in major tonality.

    15. The student sings one unfamiliar tonic major pattern.

    16. The student sings one unfamiliar dominant major pattern.

Unit 4: Verbal Association
(All singing is done with solfège syllables)

Sequential Objectives:

17. The student sings the resting tone in minor tonality *(la)*. (The patterns the teacher sings must be dominant minor, then tonic minor ending on the resting tone.)
18. The student recognizes patterns with the syllables *la, do,* and *mi* as tonic minor patterns.
19. The student recognizes patterns with the syllables *si, ti, re,* and *mi* as dominant minor patterns.
20. The student discriminates between tonic minor patterns and dominant minor patterns.
21. The students name the harmonic functions of the following tonic minor and dominant minor patterns:
    1. Tonic minor/Dominant minor;
    2. Dominant minor/Tonic minor.
22. The student sings tonic minor patterns.
23. The student sings dominant minor patterns.

Unit 5: Generalization-Verbal
(The teacher sings with a neutral syllable; the students sing with solfège syllables.)

Sequential Objectives:

24. The student identifies the harmonic functions of one familiar and one unfamiliar pattern in minor tonality.
25. The student sings one unfamiliar tonic minor pattern.
26. The student sings one unfamiliar dominant minor pattern.

136

Unit 6: Aural/Oral
(All singing is done with a neutral syllable.)

Sequential Objectives:

27. The student sings the resting tone of patterns in major tonality. (The patterns the teacher sings must be subdominant major, dominant major, then tonic major *not* ending on the resting tone.)
28. The student sings subdominant major patterns.
29. The student sings the resting tone of patterns in minor tonality. (The patterns the teacher sings must be subdominant minor, dominant minor, then tonic minor *not* ending on the resting tone.)
30. The student sings subdominant minor patterns.

Unit 7: Verbal Association
(All singing is done with solfège syllables)

Sequential Objectives:

31. The student sings the resting tone of patterns in major tonality. (The patterns the teacher sings must be subdominant major, dominant major, then tonic major *not* ending on the resting tone.)
32. The student recognizes patterns with the syllables *fa, la, and do* as subdominant major patterns.
33. The student sings subdominant major patterns.
34. The student sings the resting tone of patterns in minor tonality. (The patterns the teacher sings must be subdominant minor, dominant minor, then tonic minor *not* ending on the resting tone.)
35. The student recognizes patterns with the syllables *re, fa, and la* as subdominant minor patterns.

36. The student sings subdominant minor patterns.

Unit 8: Creativity
(All singing is done with a neutral syllable.)

Sequential Objectives:

37. The student creates and sings with a neutral syllable *any* pattern in response to a subdominant major pattern and a tonic major pattern.
38. The student creates and sings with a neutral syllable *any* pattern in response to a dominant major pattern and a tonic major pattern.
39. The student creates and sings with a neutral syllable *any* pattern in response to a subdominant minor pattern and a tonic minor pattern.
40. The student creates and sings with a neutral syllable *any* pattern in response to a dominant minor pattern and a tonic minor pattern.

Unit 9: Partial Synthesis

Sequential Objectives:

41. The student names the tonality of a series of familiar tonic, dominant, and subdominant patterns in either major or minor tonality. (The teacher uses solfège syllables.)
42. The student names the tonality of a series of familiar tonic, dominant, and subdominant patterns in either major or minor tonality. (The teacher uses a neutral syllable.)

43. The student names and compares the tonalities of two consecutive series of familiar patterns in major or minor tonality. (The teacher sings with a neutral syllable.)

Unit 10: Generalization-Verbal
(The teacher sings with a neutral syllable; the students sing with solfège syllables.)

Sequential Objectives:

44. The student identifies a series of familiar and unfamiliar tonic, dominant, and subdominant patterns as being in either major or minor tonality.

45. The student names and compares the tonalities of two consecutive series of familiar and unfamiliar patterns in major or minor tonality.

46. The student sings the resting tone of a series of familiar and unfamiliar tonic, dominant, and subdominant patterns in either major or minor tonality.

47. The student sings one unfamiliar subdominant major pattern and one unfamiliar tonic major pattern.

48. The student sings one unfamiliar dominant major pattern and one unfamiliar tonic major pattern.

49. The student sings one unfamiliar subdominant minor pattern and one unfamiliar tonic minor pattern.

50. The student sings one unfamiliar dominant minor pattern and one unfamiliar tonic minor pattern.

Unit 11: Improvisation
(All singing is done with solfège syllables.)

Sequential Objectives:

51. The student sings a tonic major pattern in response to a tonic major pattern.

52. The student sings a dominant major pattern in response to a dominant major pattern.

53. The student sings a tonic minor pattern in response to a tonic minor pattern.

54. The student sings a dominant minor pattern in response to a dominant minor pattern.

55. The student sings a dominant major and a tonic major pattern in response to a dominant major and a tonic major pattern sung by the teacher.

56. The student sings a dominant minor and a tonic minor pattern in response to a dominant minor and a tonic minor pattern sung by the teacher.

57. The student sings a subdominant major, a dominant major, and a tonic major pattern in response to a subdominant major, a dominant major, and a tonic major pattern sung by the teacher.

58. The student sings a subdominant minor, a dominant minor, and a tonic minor pattern in response to a subdominant minor, a dominant minor, and a tonic minor pattern sung by the teacher.

59. The student sings five tonic major pitches while the teacher sings five different tonic major pitches in harmony.

60. The student sings four dominant major pitches and three tonic major pitches while the teacher sings the same harmonic functions in harmony.

61. The student sings four subdominant major pitches, four dominant major pitches, and five tonic major pitches

while the teacher sings the same harmonic functions in harmony.

62. The student sings five tonic minor pitches while the teacher sings five different tonic minor pitches in harmony.

63. The student sings four dominant minor pitches and three tonic minor pitches while the teacher sings the same functions in harmony.

64. The student sings four subdominant minor pitches, four dominant minor pitches, and five tonic minor pitches while the teacher sings the same harmonic functions in harmony.

Rhythm Units and Comprehensive Objectives

Unit 1—Aural/Oral (Exercises 1-11)
Objective: Students will chant and move to macro and micro beats in duple and triple meters. All chanting will be done with a neutral syllable.

Unit 2—Verbal Association (Exercises 12-18)
Objective: Students will name the functions of the duple patterns they were taught in Unit 1 and chant them with beat-function syllables.

Unit 3—Verbal Association (Exercises 19-25)
Objective: Students will name the functions of the triple patterns they were taught in Unit 1 and chant them with beat-function syllables.

Unit 4—Aural/Oral (Exercises 26-29)
Objective: Students will move to macro beats while chanting macro beat, micro beat, and division patterns in duple meter. All chanting will be done with a neutral syllable.

Unit 5—Verbal Association (Exercises 30-36)
Objective: Students will name the functions of the patterns they were taught in Unit 4 and chant them with beat-function syllables.

Unit 6—Creativity-Aural/Oral (Exercises 37-39)
Objective: Students will create patterns in response to macro beat, micro beat, and division patterns in duple meter. All chanting will be done with a neutral syllable.

Unit 7—Aural/Oral (Exercises 40-43)
Objective: Students will move to macro beats while chanting macro beat, micro beat, and division patterns in triple meter. All chanting will be done with a neutral syllable.

Unit 8—Verbal Association (Exercises 44-49)

Objective: Students will name the functions of the patterns they were taught in Unit 7 and chant them with beat-function syllables.

Unit 9—Creativity-Aural/Oral (Exercises 50-52)

Objective: Students will create patterns in response to macro beat, micro beat, and division patterns in triple meter. All chanting will be done with a neutral syllable.

Unit 10—Partial Synthesis (Exercises 53-55)

Objective: Students will recognize that different *series* of macro beat, micro beat, and division patterns are in duple or triple meter. The teacher selects patterns that the students learned in Units 1, 4, and 7.

Unit 11—Generalization-Verbal (Exercises 56-63)

Objective: Students will chant familiar and unfamiliar macro beat, micro beat, and division patterns in duple and triple meters. Students will chant with beat-function syllables. The teacher will chant with a neutral syllable.

Unit 12—Improvisation with Verbal Association (Exercises 64-69)

Objective: Students will improvise macro beat, micro beat, and division patterns in duple and triple meter. All chanting will be done with beat-function syllables.

Unit 1: Aural/Oral
(All chanting is done with a neutral syllable.)

Sequential Objectives:
    1. The students move in a continuous, weighty, slow-motion manner.

2. The students patsch macro beats in a variety of tempi and meters (at least duple and triple).

3. The students patsch duple micro beats.

4. The students patsch triple micro beats.

5. The students stand up and rock from side to side to macro beats in duple and triple meters.

6. The students stand up and rock from side to side to macro beats while patsching duple micro beats.

7. The students stand up and rock from side to side to macro beats while patsching triple micro beats.

8. The students chant macro beat and duple micro beat patterns while standing up and rocking from side to side to macro beats.

9. The students chant macro beat and duple micro beat patterns while patsching duple micro beats.

10. The students chant macro beat and triple micro beat patterns while standing up and rocking from side to side to macro beats.

11. The students chant macro beat and triple micro beat patterns while patsching triple micro beats.

Unit 2: Verbal Association
(All chanting is done with beat-function syllables.)

Sequential Objectives:

12. The students recognize a series of *du*s as macro beats.

13. The students recognize a series of *du—de*s as duple micro beats.

14. The students discriminate between macro beats and duple micro beats.

15. The students name the rhythmic functions of the following macro beat and duple micro beat patterns. Each set is the equivalent of four macro beats long:

     1. Macro beats/Duple micro beats;

     2. Duple micro beats/Macro beats.

16. The students chant macro beat and duple micro beat patterns while standing up and rocking from side to side to macro beats.

17. The students chant macro beat and duple micro beat patterns while patsching duple micro beats.

18. The students chant macro beat and duple micro beat patterns while patsching duple micro beats. (The teacher chants with a neutral syllable; students chant with beat-function syllables.)

Unit 3: Verbal Association
(All chanting is done with beat-function syllables.)

Sequential Objectives:

19. The students recognize a series of *du—da—di*s as triple micro beats.

20. The students discriminate between duple micro beats and triple micro beats.

21. The students discriminate between macro beats and triple micro beats.

22. The students name the rhythmic functions of the following macro beat and triple micro beat patterns. Each set is the equivalent of four macro beats long:

     1. Two macro beats/Six triple micro beats;

     2. Six triple micro beats/Two macro beats.

23. The students chant macro beat and triple micro beat patterns while standing up and rocking from side to side to macro beats.

24. The students chant macro beat and triple micro beat patterns while patsching triple micro beats.

25. The students chant macro beat and triple micro beat patterns while patsching triple micro beats. (The teacher chants with a neutral syllable; students chant with beat-function syllables.)

Unit 4: Aural/Oral
(All chanting is done with a neutral syllable.)

Sequential Objectives:
26. The students chant the equivalent of four macro beats in duple meter. The first, second, and fourth beats are macro and micro beats. The third beat is a division pattern.
27. The students chant the equivalent of four macro beats in duple meter. The first, third, and fourth beats are macro and micro beats. The second beat is a division pattern.
28. The students chant the equivalent of four macro beats in duple meter. The second, third, and fourth beats are macro and micro beats. The first beat is a division pattern.
29. The students chant the equivalent of four macro beats in duple meter. The first, second, and third beats are macro and micro beats. The fourth beat is a division pattern.

Unit 5: Verbal Association
(All chanting is done with beat-function syllables.)

Sequential Objectives:
30. The students recognize any pattern with *ta* as a division pattern.
31. The students discriminate between duple micro beats and duple divisions.
32. The students name the rhythmic functions of the following patterns in duple meter. Each set is the equivalent of

four macro beats long:
1. Two macro beats/duple divisions;
2. Duple divisions/Two macro beats;
3. Duple divisions/Four duple micro beats;
4. Four duple micro beats/Duple divisions.

33. The students chant the equivalent of four macro beats in duple meter. The first, second, and fourth beats are macro and micro beats. The third beat is a division pattern.

34. The students chant the equivalent of four macro beats in duple meter. The first, third, and fourth beats are macro and micro beats. The second beat is a division pattern.

35. The students chant the equivalent of four macro beats in duple meter. The second, third, and fourth beats are macro and micro beats. The first beat is a division pattern.

36. The students chant the equivalent of four macro beats in duple meter. The first, second, and third beats are macro and micro beats. The fourth beat is a division pattern.

Unit 6: Creativity

(All chanting is done with a neutral syllable.)

Sequential Objectives:

37. The students create patterns in response to macro beat and micro beat patterns in duple meter.

38. The students create patterns in response to macro beat, micro beat, and division patterns in duple meter.

39. The students create patterns in response to macro beat and division patterns in duple meter.

Unit 7: Aural/Oral
(All chanting is done with a neutral syllable.)

Sequential Objectives:

40. The students chant the equivalent of four macro beats in triple meter. The first, second, and fourth beats are macro and micro beats. The third beat is a division pattern.

41. The students chant the equivalent of four macro beats in triple meter. The first, third, and fourth beats are macro and micro beats. The second beat is a division pattern.

42. The students chant the equivalent of four macro beats in triple meter. The second, third, and fourth beats are macro and micro beats. The first beat is a division pattern.

43. The students chant the equivalent of four macro beats in triple meter. The first, second, and third beats are macro and micro beats. The fourth beat is a division pattern.

Unit 8: Verbal Association
(All chanting is done with beat-function syllables.)

Sequential Objectives:

44. The student discriminates between triple micro beats and triple divisions.

45. The students name the rhythmic functions of the following patterns in triple meter. Each set is the equivalent of four macro beats long:
    1. Two macro beats/Triple divisions;
    2. Triple divisions/Two macro beats;
    3. Triple divisions/Six triple micro beats;
    4. Six triple micro beats/Triple divisions.

46. The students chant the equivalent of four macro beats in triple meter. The first, second, and fourth beats are macro and micro beats. The third beat is a division pattern.

47. The students chant the equivalent of four macro beats in triple meter. The first, third, and fourth beats are macro and micro beats. The second beat is a division pattern.
48. The students chant the equivalent of four macro beats in triple meter. The second, third, and fourth beats are macro and micro beats. The first beat is a division pattern.
49. The students chant the equivalent of four macro beats in triple meter. The first, second, and third beats are macro and micro beats. The fourth beat is a division pattern.

Unit 9: Creativity
(All chanting is done with a neutral syllable.)

Sequential Objectives:
50. The students create patterns in response to macro beat and micro beat patterns in triple meter.
51. The students create patterns in response to macro beat, micro beat, and division patterns in triple meter.
52. The students create patterns in response to macro beat and division patterns in triple meter.

Unit 10: Partial Synthesis

Sequential Objectives:
53. The students name the meter of a series of familiar macro beat, micro beat, and division patterns in either duple or triple meter. (The teacher uses beat-function syllables.)
54. The students name the meter of the series of patterns used in exercise 53. (The teacher uses a neutral syllable.)
55. The students name and compare the meters of two series of patterns used in exercise 53. (The teacher uses a neutral syllable.)

Unit 11: Generalization-Verbal
(The teacher chants with a neutral syllable;
the student chants with beat-function syllables.)

Sequential Objectives:

56. The students identify the rhythmic functions of one familiar and one unfamiliar pattern in duple meter (four macro beats long).

57. The students identify the rhythmic functions of one familiar and one unfamiliar pattern in triple meter (four macro beats long).

58. The students identify a series of macro beat, micro beat, and division patterns (some familiar and some unfamiliar) as being in either duple or triple meter.

59. The students chant the underlying micro beats of a series of macro beat, micro beat, and division patterns (some familiar and some unfamiliar) in either duple or triple meter.

60. The students chant one familiar and one unfamiliar pattern made up of macro beats, duple micro beats, and divisions.

61. The students chant one familiar and one unfamiliar pattern made up of macro beats, triple micro beats, and divisions.

62. The students chant two unfamiliar macro beat, duple micro beat, and division patterns.

63. The students chant two unfamiliar macro beat, triple micro beat, and division patterns.

Unit 12: Improvisation
(All chanting is done with beat-function syllables.)

Sequential Objectives:

64. The students chant two patterns with macro beats and duple micro beats in response to two duple division patterns chanted by the teacher.

65. The students chant two duple division patterns in response to two patterns with macro beats and duple micro beats chanted by the teacher.

66. The students chant two patterns with macro beats and triple micro beats in response to two triple division patterns chanted by the teacher.

67. The students chant two triple division patterns in response to two patterns with macro beats and triple micro beats chanted by the teacher.

68. The students improvise macro, duple micro, and division patterns (the equivalent of eight macro beats) and chant them at the same time the teacher is chanting a series of duple micro beats (also the equivalent of eight macro beats).

69. The students improvise macro, triple micro, and division patterns (the equivalent of eight macro beats) and chant them at the same time the teacher is chanting a series of triple micro beats (also the equivalent of eight macro beats).

CHAPTER 12
Techniques For Teaching Patterns

"The horror of that moment," the King went on,
"I shall never, never forget!"
"You will though," the Queen said,
"if you don't make a memorandum of it."

—Lewis Carroll
Alice in Wonderland

In chapter 2, I mentioned that teachers should devise their own techniques for teaching patterns; also, they should select classroom activities that, together with pattern instruction, form the content of each lesson; finally, they should coordinate classroom activities with pattern instruction so that the two reinforce each other.

Probably, if you're an experienced music teacher, you know many appropriate classroom activities; you also can figure out for yourself how to coordinate classroom activities with pattern instruction (or "learning sequence activities" as Edwin Gordon calls them).

But how should you teach patterns? There are millions of ways. In fact, there are at least as many ways to teach patterns as there are music teachers. I'll spend the next several pages describing some techniques that work for me; but I don't want to mislead you by saying that my way is "the way."

I'll use a numbered, "do this, don't do that" format, but don't let that throw you: eventually you'll make up your own techniques and you won't be dependent on mine, Gordon's, or anyone else's.

General Techniques For Teaching Patterns

1. Gordon has suggested that a single tonal or rhythm exercise should never run longer than ten minutes. The rest of the class period should be spent on rote songs and traditional activities.

   I like this suggestion but I don't always follow it, particularly when I'm teaching rhythm patterns. Sometimes, if I sense that my students are enthusiastic and on task, I'll spend *half the period* doing nothing but call-and-response rhythm exercises. (Shh. Don't tell anybody.)

   Tonal patterns are a different story. Children have a great deal of trouble staying focused on tonal patterns for more than a few minutes. Instead of devoting a large, 10-minute chunk of time to tonal patterns, I teach them in dribs and drabs throughout a period. Two minutes here, two minutes there. (Of course I make sure to establish tonality and key each time I begin.) I tend to get better results when I teach a tonal exercise sporadically throughout the period instead of in one ten-minute chunk.

2. As I said before, these exercises are basically call-and-response activities. What you do is this: you sing or chant something; then you ask *one child at a time* to sing or chant in some specific way in response to what you just sang or chanted; and you write down whether they sang or chanted correctly.

   Gordon did not invent the call-and-response activity of course. He did add a new wrinkle to it, however: context. (Are you getting tired of hearing me say this?) Everything you sing and chant must be put in an explicit tonal or metrical context. Only this way can you replace pitch-matching, imitation, and senseless drill, with pattern matching, audiation, and meaningful—er, drill. Let's face it: pattern instruction is "drill" no matter how you slice it. How meaningful and stimulating it is depends on you! If you think it's fun, your students will think it's fun; if you think it's a pointless waste of time, so will they. (I once heard an otherwise intelligent colleague say that she'd never use the "Gordon method" because "it's boring." This is as unfair as it is stupid. Of course pattern instruction is boring *if she decides to make it boring*. Personally, I prefer to make it exciting and interesting.)

3. On the following pages you'll see a typical tonal exercise and a typical rhythm exercise. Notice that there are three different kinds of patterns in both exercises: easy, moderately difficult, and difficult (E, M, and D). The difficulty levels are based on audiation difficulty and not on performance difficulty. Even so, my experience is that the easy patterns tend to be easy for children to perform in context; the difficult patterns tend to be difficult to perform in context.[20]

4. Gordon has come up with an intriguing way of acknowledging differences in aptitude among students and accommodating their individual needs: All students, regardless of their aptitude level, perform the easy pattern first. After that, the average and high aptitude students learn the moderately difficult pattern; and then finally the students with high aptitude learn the difficult pattern. The most attractive aspect of this approach is that no child is deprived of anything. All children learn the same skills

---

20 Information about the audiation difficulty levels of hundreds of patterns can be found in the 1989 edition of *Learning Sequences in Music* by Edwin Gordon. Gordon mysteriously omitted this extremely valuable information from the 1993 edition.

and the same content, but in accordance with their level of ability.

5. How do I keep track of who's singing what? After all, some students will be working on the difficult pattern while others are still on the easy one. On the following pages, you'll see my seating charts for my two schools. (I need two different seating charts because the rooms are shaped differently.) Inside each box, I write the name of a student. Underneath the student's name I write her aptitude level (H, HA, A, LA, or L). Those three smaller boxes at the bottom of each larger box are where I keep track of the students' responses. Here's how I fill them in: **X** means they performed the pattern perfectly. **/** means they tried but didn't get it. I'll call on them later if there's time. An empty square is an empty square: I haven't called on that student yet to perform that particular pattern.

A typical square in the seating chart might look something like this:[21]

What does this mean? It means that the fictional student whom I've called Kristin Davis has high-average aptitude and has already performed the easy pattern correctly, but is still working on the moderately difficult pattern.

---

21 These techniques for evaluation are almost identical to those that Gordon uses in the revised edition of *Jump Right In: The Music Curriculum.* I find it a remarkable coincidence that I came up with these ideas independently of—and before—Gordon. Then again, perhaps it is not such a remarkable coincidence; perhaps these techniques are an inevitable simplification of the first edition of *Jump Right In.*

Tonal Exercise 7

1. Sing the major introductory sequence in F with solfège syllables.
2. Sing the appropriate set of patterns written below with solfège syllables.
3. Call on one student to sing.
4. The student sings, with solfège syllables, only the last pitch of the pattern.
5. Continue to call on individual students and re-establish tonality from time to time.

(Class patterns should start with a dominant pattern and end with a tonic pattern. The resting tone should be the final note.)

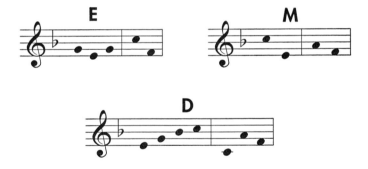

Rhythm Exercise 23

1. You and your students stand up and rock from side to side on the macro beats (the dotted quarter note pulse) with a consistent tempo.
2. Chant one of the three sets of patterns written below with beat-function syllables.
3. On the fourth macro beat, pick one student to chant the set of patterns in echo. (Because you're chanting, you must

use hand gestures and eye contact to bring the student in on the fifth macro beat.)

4. The student chants the patterns in echo.

(Class patterns should include both macro and micro beats.)

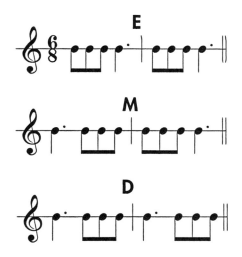

Room_____

Exercise_____

Room_____

Exercise_____

Specific Techniques For Teaching Tonal Patterns

1. Before you begin most of the tonal exercises, you must establish tonality. It's best to do that with your voice rather than with a piano. You don't have to sing a particular sequence of pitches; any song without words will do. I tend to sing melodies—that is, I combine the tonal and rhythm elements when I establish tonality in spite of what Gordon recommends. My experience is that children respond better this way. Of course, once I start teaching tonal patterns, I sing without melodic rhythm.

2. This is a good way to establish major tonality:

Do Re Mi Fa   So La So   So Fa Re Ti   Do   Mi   Do

3. This is a good way to establish minor tonality:

La Ti Do Re   Mi Fa Mi   Mi Re Ti Si   La Do La

4. Gordon has suggested that "bum" makes a good neutral syllable to sing with. I tend to use both "bum" and "bah."

5. Just a reminder: You shouldn't add any rhythmic elements to the tonal patterns. The patterns should be sung in a tempo but not in a meter.

6. Sing in a separated, not connected style.

7. Another reminder: If the exercise calls for you to use tonal syllables, use the movable *do* system, with *do*-based major and *la*-based minor.

8. You might occasionally want the whole class to sing together. I generally start by singing at least two or three patterns for the whole class to sing back, just to get everybody warmed up. From then on, I use one of these "class" patterns after three or four individual responses. (When you perform a class pattern, don't forget to motion for the whole class to respond together. Give some kind of prepartory beat with a breath and then a downbeat.) One more thing: it's best if you make up a few class patterns before your students come to you. Be creative.

9. Here's how to do it:
    • Sing
    • Wait a second or two. (Try not to make this second or two metrical.)This pause encourages students to audiate rather than imitate.
    • Breathe with the student while raising your arm to indicate an upbeat.
    • Then lower your arm to indicate a downbeat. The downbeat you give should be pretty vigorous.
    • The students should sing on that downbeat.

Specific Techniques For Teaching Rhythm Patterns

1. You don't have to establish tempo and meter with an introductory sequence. Just start moving and chanting in the tempo and meter you want and ask the kids to join in.
2. Once again: Don't add any tonal elements to the rhythm exercises—that is, just chant the rhythms without singing them. Use lots of vocal inflection as you would in speech.
3. These exercises should be done in place, not around the room "in space."
4. If the exercise calls for you to chant with a neutral sylla-

ble, use "bah." This is Gordon's suggestion and I think it's a good one. Again, I tend to alternate between "bum" and "bah" depending on the melodic rhythm of the patterns I'm chanting.

5. You might occasionally want the whole class to chant together. As with the tonal exercises, I generally start by chanting at least two or three patterns for the whole class to respond to, just to get everybody warmed up. From then on, I use one of these "class" patterns after three or four individual responses.

6. Once again: If the exercise calls for you to use rhythm syllables, use the beat-function syllable system.

7. Here's how you do it:
   - Chant.
   - Make eye contact with the student who's about to chant after you.
   - On your fourth macro beat, show with a free hand that the student is to breathe.
   - The student breathes on the final upbeat and then chants the patterns on the next downbeat.

8. Important: DON'T STOP! This is, don't interrupt the flow of the rhythm to give your students "time to think." This would destroy the sense of tempo and meter that you've worked so hard to establish.

   Look at it this way: When you sing tonal patterns, you can pause for a second or two to give your students "audiation time." All you need to do to maintain tonal syntax is alternate between tonic and dominant functions so that students can relate patterns to a resting tone; on the other hand, you can maintain rhythm syntax only through a continuity of sound. So keep those rhythm patterns going at all costs!

9. You should be relaxed and free as you move during these

exercises. Gordon has a great saying: "Dance with yourself!"

Odds and Ends

1. Keep things moving. Don't dwell too long on any single child.
2. The tonal and rhythm exercises have nothing to do with each other. The class could be on rhythm exercise 22 and tonal exercise 15.
3. It's best if you *don't* do a tonal and a rhythm exercise during the same period—for a total of twenty minutes—even if you think the children can handle it. Do one or the other during a single class period. I generally alternate every two weeks.
4. Certainly don't tell your students the names of notes such as "quarter note," "eighth note," "B flat," "F sharp." Stick to syllables.
5. Move your class on to the next exercise when about 80% of the class can do the patterns correctly. This is another of Gordon's suggestions. I like it.
6. Never move *part* of a class on to the next exercise. They all must move together.
7. You'll be lucky if you finish one exercise in one period. Probably you'll finish only part of an exercise in one period. Don't worry about that; tomorrow's another day. Just make sure you keep a record of how far your students got.

A Few Closing Thoughts

I hope you're not saying to yourself: "This is too much for me. I'll never understand Music Learning Theory fully. And I'll never be able to write a curriculum based on it."

I understand how overwhelming it may seem. Still, my advice is: GO AHEAD AND WRITE A CURRICULUM ANYWAY! As you gradually put together your own set of sequential objectives and units, you'll find that your understanding of Music Learning Theory will grow.

"But I don't think I will ever understand it fully!" you may still be saying. Well, neither will I. Neither will Edwin Gordon. Neither will *anyone*. Don't let that stop you. Keep growing! Certainly there are a lot of sources you can go to for more information. (If you think I've put a lot of information into this book, you'll be amazed to discover how much I left out.)

Another thing: Give yourself time. As Richard Simmons once said about exercise, "Start slow but start *now*." And don't be afraid to make mistakes. Darrel Walters put it this way: "Teachers will continue to make their share of mistakes and misjudgments, and students, pliable as they are, will continue to learn."

And don't forget some of the benefits you'll see and hear in your classroom. Imagine a whole class of second graders saying "Triple Meter" when you play a piece in class that they've never heard before. Imagine your third graders understanding music better than your second graders. Imagine fourth graders who are *ready* to begin studying a musical instrument. Imagine each class sounding like a choir. And imagine your choir sounding like heaven!

Yes, yes, I know. It's time to return to earth. *Of course* none of these things will happen overnight. But that doesn't mean that they won't happen at all. Imagine one more thing: Someday your students will grow musically to the point where they won't be your students anymore. They will be your colleagues. And that will be the greatest tribute to your success as a teacher.

Bibliography

Atterbury, Betty W. 1992. "Research on the Teaching of Elementary General Music." In R. Colwell (Ed.), *Handbook Of Research On Music Teaching And Learning.* New York: Schirmer Books.

Bernstein, Leonard. 1966. *The Infinite Variety of Music.* New York: Simon and Schuster.

Bernstein, Leonard. 1976. *The Unanswered Question: Six Talks At Harvard.* Cambridge, Massachusetts: Harvard University Press.

Bernstein, Leonard. 1992. *Leonard Bernstein's Young People's Concerts.* New York: Bantam Doubleday Dell Publishing Group.

Buscaglia, Leo F. 1984. *Loving Each Other: The Challenge of Human Relationships.* New York: Ballantine Books.

Chall, Jeanne S. 1967. *Learning To Read: The Great Debate.* New York: McGraw-Hill.

Chall, Jeanne S. 1983. *Stages Of Reading Development.* New York: McGraw-Hill.

Colwell, Richard and Abrahams, Frank. 1991. "Edwin Gordon's Contributions: An Appraisal." *The Quarterly*, II, 1 and 2, pp. 19-35.

Dean, Roger. 1989. "Teacher Education and Music Learning Theory." In D. L. Walters and C. C. Taggart (Eds.), *Readings in Music Learning Theory.* Chicago: G.I.A.

Ehri, Linnea C., Barron, Roderick W., and Feldman, Jeffrey M. 1978. *The Recognition Of Words.* Newark, Delaware: International Reading Association.

Flesch, Rudolf. 1951. *The Art of Clear Thinking.* New York: Harper and Row.

Flesch, Rudolf. 1954. *How To Make Sense.* New York: Harper and Brothers.

Flesch, Rudolf. 1955. *Why Johnny Can't Read—And What You Can Do About It.* New York: Harper and Row.

Flesch, Rudolf. 1981. *Why Johnny Still Can't Read.* New York: Harper and Row.

Gordon, Edwin E. 1982. *Intermediate Measures of Music Audiation.* Chicago: G.I.A

Gordon, Edwin E. and Woods, David G. 1986. *Jump Right In: The Music Curriculum.* Chicago: G.I.A.

Gordon, Edwin E. 1987. *The Nature, Description, Measurement, and Evaluation of Music Aptitudes.* Chicago: G.I.A.

Gordon, Edwin E. 1989. *Learning Sequences in Music.* Chicago: G.I.A.

Gordon, Edwin E. 1990. *A Music Learning Theory for Newborn and Young Children.* Chicago: G.I.A.

Gordon Edwin E. 1991. "A Response to Volume II, Numbers 1 and 2 of the Quarterly." *The Quarterly*, II (4), pp. 62-72.

Gordon, Edwin E. 1993. *Learning Sequences in Music.* Chicago: G.I.A.

Gurren, Louise, and Hughes, Ann. 1965. "Intensive Phonics vs. Gradual Phonics in Beginning Reading: A Review." *Journal of Educational Research.* 58 (8) (April): pp. 339-346.

Keller, Helen. 1980. *The Story of My Life.* U.S.A.: Watermill Press. (Originally published in 1902)

Kushner, Harold S. 1981. *When Bad Things Happen To Good People.* New York: Schocken Books.

Laubach, Frank C. 1945. *The Silent Billion Speak.* New York: Friendship Press.

Leacock, Stephen. 1943. *How To Write.* New York: Dodd, Mead, and Company.

Mason, Lowell. 1838. *Manual for the Boston Academy of Music for Instruction in the Elements of Vocal Music, on the System of Pestalozzi.* Boston: J. H. Wilkins and R. B. Carter.

Nimoy, Leonard. 1975. *I Am Not Spock.* California: Celestial Arts.

Samuels, S. Jay. 1971. "Letter-Name vs. Letter-Sound Knowledge In Learning To Read." *The Reading Teacher.* 24 (7) (April): pp. 604-608.

Seeger, Peter. 1973. *Henscratches and Flyspecks.* New York: Berkley Publishing Corporation.

Smith, Frank. 1979. "Conflicting Approaches To Reading Research And Instruction." In Resnick, Lauren B., and Weaver, P. A., eds. *Theory and Practice of Early Reading.* Hillsdale, New Jersey: Lawrence Erlbaum Associates. vol. 2.

Smith, Frank. 1985. *Reading Without Nonsense.* New York: Teachers College Press.

Smith, Frank. 1988. *Understanding Reading.* Hillsdale: Lawrence Erlbaum Associates.

Walcutt, Charles C., Lamport, J., and McCracken, G. 1974. *Teaching Reading.* New York: Macmillan. (Chapters on research and evaluation by Robert Dykstra.)

Walters, Darrel L. 1987. "Coordinating Classroom Activities and Learning Sequence Activities." Chicago: G.I.A.

Walters, Darrel L. 1989. "Coordinating Learning Sequence Activities and Classroom Activities." In D. L. Walters and C. C. Taggart (Eds.), *Readings in Music Learning Theory.* Chicago: G.I.A.

Walters, Darrel L. 1991. "Edwin Gordon's Music Aptitude Work." *The Quarterly,* II, 1 and 2, pp. 65-72.

Walters, Darrel L. 1992. "Sequencing For Efficient Learning." In R. Colwell (Ed.), *Handbook Of Research On Music Teaching And Learning.* New York: Schirmer Books.

Wepman, Joseph M. 1964. "The Perceptual Basis for Learning." In Robinson, H. Alan (Ed.) *Meeting Individual Differences in Reading.* University of Chicago Press, Supplementary Educational Monographs, no. 94, December, pp. 25-33.

About the Author

Eric Bluestine attended Oberlin College and Temple University where he studied piano with George Sementovsky. For the past six years, he has been an elementary school music teacher in the Philadelphia public school system. He is also on the faculty of the Music Preparatory Division of Temple University where he teaches music to preschool children.